Aug. 13, 1976

To: Romeo.

I hope that this book will
be of some benefit to you
in planning and organizing
your objectives. Remember,
nothing is so empty as a
day or life without a
purpose and plan.

yours,
Randy

MODERN TECHNIQUES OF SUPERVISION

MODERN
TECHNIQUES
OF
SUPERVISION

By

ALFRED LATEINER

LATEINER PUBLISHING
6040 Boulevard East
West New York, N. J. 07093

To Jeannine

CONTENTS

Contents

INTRODUCTION

AT THE BEGINNING OF THIS CENTURY the foreman
was considered a vital part of management. Often
he alone was responsible for running the shop. He
hired and fired at will, set hours and wages, kept
time, and controlled production. His word was
final, and even the company president or owner
hesitated before questioning his actions.

As companies grew in size and complexity, however, the picture changed. A major factor was the
growth of unionism. Little by little the supervisor's
duties and powers were chipped away. His position lost some of its importance and prestige. De-
signing and setting up new machinery, developing
new synthetic materials, working out improved production — these called for the engineer and other
trained specialists. The authority of the supervisor
over his men was undercut. Hiring was taken over
by the personnel manager, and as unions introduced
the idea of shop stewards or "shop committee chair-
men," the once all-powerful foreman was no longer
free to deal with his men as he wished.

Management did little to help the situation. It
frequently bypassed the foreman and dealt directly
with the worker or the union representative on matters such as discipline, announcing work schedules,
and pay raises.

As authority and responsibility were split off in
many directions, the morale and efficiency of the

worker, as well as of the supervisor, began to suffer. "I have fourteen bosses and each of them tells me something different" was a common employee complaint.

Management began to realize that bypassing and weakening the authority of the supervisor had been a mistake. There was still an important place for him in the company setup; in fact he was the key man in the productive effort. If a plant or office were to operate efficiently, responsibility for leading the group must be given to one person. Obviously the individual to do this job was the supervisor. Management knew, however, that going back to the old system of making the supervisor an absolute boss was impossible. Companies had become too big and complicated for this. Executives began to ask themselves, "What is to be the real function of the 'middle-manager'?"

Today many firms are coming up with the answer. Instead of giving the supervisor power to set policy, they give him authority to *interpret* it to the men under him. He is the funnel through which management, engineers, and other specialists reach the employee. Regulations, policies, and methods are first worked out by the executives and technicians. Then they are given to the foreman who, in turn, applies them in dealing with his men. In this way the supervisor's job becomes a sort of "clearing agency" to avoid confusion and divided responsibility. A clear channel of communication is provided.

As many of the supervisor's duties and responsibilities have been restored, his prestige has begun to rise once more. His job is considered a professional position requiring experience and training. Many companies are conducting training courses for foremen and supervisors to help them develop skill and understanding in the various phases of the job of supervision. Common topics used in training conferences are accident prevention, job instruction, human relations, methods improvement (work simplification), quality control, waste reduction, company history, and community relations.

How the Supervisor is Selected

It is a tradition in American business and industry to choose a supervisor for one of two reasons: either because he has been on the job a long time, or because he is an expert worker. In unionized shops the line of promotion is often covered in labor agreements. In companies in which the work requires employees with special or highly trained skills, the man who is chosen to be a supervisor usually has shown himself to be a skilled worker. In a stenographic office, for example, the best secretary may be appointed office manager. A foreman in a machine shop must be, first of all, an expert machinist. The head salesman or sales manager of a firm may have shown that he can outsell the other salesmen.

The supervisor who is chosen because he is an expert usually falls into one of two types: he may be an "old-timer" who has gained all or most of his skill through practical experience, or he may be a younger man whose knowledge came largely through formal education. Among the latter group is the chemist promoted to supervisor in a firm that manufactures drug products, or the junior executive in a department store appointed to a supervisory position because he studied retailing in college. There are cases, of course, when a company cannot help itself and is forced to look to the outside to fill openings. This is especially true where the firm needs a highly trained technician or specialist. A large food company may look in vain among its own men for a skilled chemist to supervise its research department, and end up recruiting someone from the outside.

Although it is only fair for the company to consider employee performance or length of service when making promotions from within, this should not be the only yardstick. Just because an employee has been with the company for a long time doesn't necessarily mean that he will make a good supervisor. There is also no guarantee that an employee who shows himself to be a qualified worker has the qualities needed to be a good boss. One question to take into account is: "Will this person be able to serve the organization as well in the new job?" A mistake can be costly. If the employee turns out to be a poor supervisor the company suffers because it now has a poor leader on its hands, and it has also lost a man who may have been a valuable worker, since demotion is not practical.

A supervisor should be chosen because he blends a number of different qualities. He must know his company's policies and philosophy and should have experience and knowledge of the work itself. He must be able to understand and handle people. He should be informed on labor laws and union agreements. He must know how to instruct workers. He must be able to keep records and improve work methods. He should be a bit of engineer, psychologist, teacher, accountant, and industrial expert.

To put it another way, what good is it if the foreman in a bakery knows how to mix dough well if he can't get the workers under him to mix it right? A supervisor draws his salary not only because he can do a job well, but because of his ability to get others to do it well.

The advantages of promoting from within the ranks are clear. Unlike the class or "caste" systems in other countries, promotion is based on the democratic principle of recognizing a man for what he does rather than who he is. It is a principle that Americans have been taught since childhood — one that the employee in this country can grasp and understand. The employee or supervisor will be more conscientious and efficient when he knows that succeeding in his job will place him in line for further promotions. His morale, as well as the morale of those under him, will be higher. Everyone feels that he is a vital member of the company family.

"Are good bosses born or made?" A boss may seem to have been born to the job of supervision. He has a natural gift for handling people and has all the other qualities needed to make a good boss. For most of us, however, the ability to supervise is not an inborn trait. It must be developed through experience and training. Almost any experienced person who learns the principles of supervision and combines these principles with a liberal dose of common sense will have little trouble filling the supervisory role.

Alfred Lateiner

MODERN TECHNIQUES OF SUPERVISION

UNDERSTANDING AND DEALING
WITH PEOPLE

As a supervisor your job is to obtain certain results. This includes turning out sufficient work of good quality. What's more, you must turn it out within a given time, or according to a schedule. You must also give reasonable care to equipment and conserve materials. You must prevent accidents and job interruptions. Most important of all, you must see to it that the good results you get are continued.

These are things you are responsible for to management. Yet they can only be accomplished through the people under you. Your success depends entirely on them. With their help you can achieve results; without it you will fail.

Consider what happened in a large factory not long ago when the supervisors went out on strike, but the employees didn't. Despite the lack of supervisory help, production continued at a reasonable level. What would have happened if the situation had been reversed — if the employees had walked out instead? The answer is obvious: production would have been seriously crippled.

The supervisor is often referred to as the "middleman." This is a good way of putting it. You are indeed a buffer between management and employees. You are like the person in the middle when

three people squeeze into the front seat of a car —
you are pressed in from both sides.

It is up to you, therefore, to work out an approach
to your supervisory job that will enable all three
passengers in the company machine — labor, top
management, and you — to travel smoothly and
comfortably.

You can do this by being a boss without bossing
people; by leading instead of pushing the men and
women you supervise; by getting them to pitch in
willingly; by giving an employee the feeling that
he, too, has a big stake in the company.

It's up to you to decide what type of boss you're
going to be. Are you going to be the supervisor who
tries to force action and behavior, working on the
employees' fear of rank and authority? Or are you
going to persuade and lead people to do what they
should do?

Remember, the difference between pushing and
leading is that when you push a worker he'll stop
working the moment you turn your back. But when
you use your persuasive powers and get him to do
things willingly, you can be reasonably certain that
he will continue to work when your back is turned.

In order to deal with people successfully, you first
have to understand them. You must understand
their needs, their feelings, their likes and dislikes.
You have to consider how and why people behave
as they do. You must learn what makes them "tick."

Are people alike or different? This is like asking
you whether the following fractions are alike or different: $\frac{1}{4}$ $\frac{2}{4}$ $\frac{3}{4}$.

These three fractions are not exactly alike. They
are different above the lines. But underneath the

lines they have something in common. They are all "fourths." You may recall from your school days that the figure "4" underneath the line in this example is referred to as the "common denominator."

The same thing is true of people. No two are exactly alike. Yet they all have certain "common denominators" of behavior. By understanding these similarities you will know certain things that apply to all employees. These laws of behavior will be true of the people who work for you. They will also be true of the workers in the next department and of the men or women you haven't laid eyes on yet, but who may work for you tomorrow, next week, next month, or in the distant future.

However, knowing laws of behavior that apply to people in general is not enough. Human beings, like our mathematical fractions, have individual differences, and you should be able to judge employees on individual differences as well as on the common denominators of behavior.

How People Differ

People are different in three areas: In the way they *think;* in the way they *feel;* in the way they *act.*

Think refers to the individual's mental traits — his intelligence, his ability to think logically, his ability to "catch on"; his thinking habits.

Feel refers to emotional traits — a person's reaction to criticism, his aggressiveness, how quickly he gets angry; his emotional habits.

Act refers to muscular traits — the individual's bodily strength, stamina, quickness of movement, coordination; his "doing" habits.

Judging individual differences is not always easy. It requires observation and experience. But as you develop skill in sizing up and appraising people, you will find that handling employees can be a much easier task than you imagined.

How People Are Alike

There are certain needs, desires, and traits that are present in all of us. These cause the common denominators of human behavior mentioned earlier. They are as true of the South Sea Island native as they are of the secretary in an office, the salesgirl behind a counter, or the worker in a factory. Some of these similarities are:

1. The "Group Instinct"

It has always been natural for people to want to "herd" together. They want to be with other human beings. They want to be associated with some group or groups. This has been true at all times and in all places. It is true of the workers under you and of the executives over you. It is true of you, your wife, your children, and your next door neighbors.

2. Resistance to Change

The laws of physics say that once an object is traveling in a given direction, force must be applied to change the direction. The more sudden and distinct the change, the greater the force which is required. You can see an example of this in driving your car. Let's assume you are going along a road and make a sharp turn. You notice there is resistance. The steering wheel tends to "fight back." If the turn is too sharp, you may even go into a skid, lose control of the car, and wind up in an accident. But if you make the turn a slow one, you will find you can accomplish it easily, gently, and safely.

This principle holds true in handling human beings. Once people do things in a certain way, they form muscular and mental habits. Changing their muscular habits and ways of thinking must be done gradually. It requires patient effort. If you help them make the change gradually, less effort is needed than if the "change of direction" is sharp. If the change is too sudden there is the danger that people, like automobiles, will rebel at your control.

Assume, for example, that your grocer decides to raise the price of milk by five cents. If he's experienced, he knows that increasing the price a nickel overnight will anger his customers and cause them to take their business elsewhere. He may raise the price only one cent at first and explain that higher costs have made the increase necessary. When he's sure you are accustomed to this increase, he'll raise it again, and so on.

The same is true in other situations. Take a union demand for wage increases. A smart labor leader knows that asking for a sudden large pay raise will only meet with resistance on the part of management and the general public. He spaces his demands and makes them gradually. He recognizes that in this way he has a better chance of succeeding.

3. *Ego-Hunger*

All of us want to be important. For a human being, the point around which the world turns is a spot that can be indicated by holding a pencil over the center of his head. When a person bruises his finger,

the pain is all-important to him. It may be more
important to him at the moment than the death of
several hundred people in some distant earthquake.

What is "ego"? It means "I"; and "I" is one of
the most important words in our vocabulary. A survey has been made of words most commonly used
over the telephone. "I," the shortest in the English
language, turned out to be the one used most often.

John Dewey, the famous philosopher, once said:
"The desire to be important is the strongest urge in
human nature." Thus, "ego-hunger" is a vital factor in handling people. It leads us to some basic
rules of human relations. One of these is that *it's
natural for people to resent criticism.* That's why
you'll find it's easy to make people dislike you when
you belittle them, ignore them, reprimand them in
front of fellow-employees, or fail to give them praise
when it is earned. Such blows to the ego cannot
be taken lightly. In order to deal with people skillfully, you must learn to respect their egos by seeing
things from their viewpoint as well as your own.

4.   *Desire for Security*

If you were to ask a number of people what
"security" is, the answer given most often would be,
"Money in the bank." Such an answer is simple.
But it is also misleading. Security is a state of mind.
It is not a condition. A better way of defining it
is to say that security is the feeling of self-confidence
and calm inner strength that comes with peace of
mind. Money alone does not guarantee peace of
mind. A dependable worker who is sure of his skill
and whose job and way of living give him a feeling
of purpose has a great deal of security.

What factors make for security? A good way to find out is to imagine yourself stranded on a South Sea island. What would you need to give you peace of mind and security?

In his work with supervisors the author makes it a point to ask the above question. The answers received usually show a surprising amount of agreement. They are the answers that you might give.

a) Food would obviously be your first interest. You would look around for something to eat — coconuts, perhaps — and a spring to supply you with water.

b) Protection would be your next concern. Once you knew where your meals were coming from, you would want a place to sleep, a covering to protect you from the winds and rain, clothing to keep you warm, a fire to frighten away animals.

c) Companionship would be your third desire. You would want to have contact with other human beings. You would want friends; someone to talk to, people to live with.

d) Next, you would want greater comfort. You might decide to build a softer bed, a larger shelter, furniture, and maybe an irrigation ditch to enable you to obtain water more easily.

e) Finally, you would want the satisfaction of knowing that other people on the island respect you. To win this respect and approval, you might try to become their leader. If you were not aggressive, you might seek other means to get them to think well of you. You might offer to help your neighbors build their shelters. You might even volunteer to carry out some task which, although disagreeable, is necessary for the good of all.

Let's shift the scene. Instead of a small imaginary island, let's take a large area — the United States. Instead of a few people, we are now dealing with more than 200 million.

Are the factors that make for peace of mind and security changed? Examine the above list carefully. A little thought shows that they aren't. Food, protection, social life, comfort, and the approval of others are universal needs. They are sought by the factory employee and white-collar worker as well as by the individual stranded on a deserted island.

American resources, technical know-how, and mass production guarantee us a reasonable amount of food, shelter, clothing, and protection against natural enemies. Since we usually live and work in close contact with other men and women, companionship is possible. Our high standard of living makes it possible for the average worker to enjoy such comforts as automobiles, refrigerators, boats, television, and up-to-date plumbing.

The old saying, "Man does not live by bread alone," seems to be especially true in the case of most Americans. The average citizen in this country spends a great deal of time and effort winning the approval of people.

Proof of this is seen in most of our daily actions. Americans, for example, give more money to charity than any other people. We are the most fashion-conscious nation on earth. We probably use more cosmetics, deodorants, and toothpaste than the rest of the world combined.

Even the person who claims he doesn't care "what other people think" is no exception. On the contrary, it's safe to assume that this man or woman is even more in need of approval than the rest of us. We have all run into such individuals. He may be the fellow who likes to boast about how many traffic rules he breaks. He may be the guest at a party who, for no apparent reason, insults everyone he meets. He may be the person who wears loud or unusual clothes in public. These people break rules the rest of the group accept because, by "being different," they hope to win approval.

How can understanding all the factors that make for a feeling of security help you as a supervisor?

Too many supervisors mistakenly cling to the idea that money in the bank and security are one and the same thing. They assume that cash alone is what the employee is interested in. They overlook his need for approval. They fail to see that the American employee today has reached the point where his acceptance by his group and leader is as important to his peace of mind and security as a paycheck.

The alert supervisor doesn't make this error. He uses the need for approval to advantage. He knows that a rulebook doesn't mean a thing if employees refuse to abide by it. Posting a rule against smoking, for example, is worthless if workers don't see the need for it and continue smoking. In a plant that makes explosives, such a rule isn't even necessary. The danger is so clear that the group as a whole readily accepts the need to curb smoking. And woe be unto the individual worker who decides to smoke anyway. He will immediately lose favor among his associates — assuming that they don't take even stronger measures.

You can apply this principle in dealing with the "problem employee." Almost every supervisor has

run into the worker who boasts that he doesn't care
what anyone thinks and breaks rules or disrupts
routine by playing the part of a "cutup." In most
cases, this type of employee, like the person who
wears gaudy clothes, is actually trying to gain attention. He is desperately in need of approval. You
can put his desire for approval to work in more prof-
itable ways. Find out what he likes to do and does
best. Emphasize his strong points in front of other
employees. Encourage him to win the attention and
approval he craves by legitimate means.

"Supervisory Climate" is Important

Many supervisors, faced with a series of personnel
problems, are quick to throw up their hands in dis-
gust and blame their headaches on the workers.
They take the attitude, "I can't do a thing with my
men. They don't know and they don't seem to care."

Such supervisors are convinced that the only solution is to get better employees. They spend most of
their time and effort complaining about the faults
of their men. They keep looking forward to the day
when they'll find the "perfect" employee. Yet he
never seems to appear. They are surprised to find
that each new worker is as bad, if not worse, than
his predecessor. In addition to a poor production
record, this type of supervisor is also noted for the
high employee turnover in his department.

His mistake, of course, is in worrying about a
change of personnel in a situation that probably
calls for a change in supervisory "climate." He fails
to see that developing good employee attitudes depends on his proper handling of the men he already

has, instead of looking for the "perfect employee."
He would do well to heed the advice of a famous
chef who once said: "It's not the potatoes you pick
but how they're cooked that's important."

You play a key role in the building of a healthy
company climate. This holds true even when the
executives who head your company believe in a
"tough" employee relations policy. How you handle
your subordinates is, to some degree, up to you.
You represent the company to the employees
under you. Employee attitudes in your group are
mainly the product of the climate you set in your
own department.

It's also important to remember that the supervisory climate, if it is to be a healthy one, must be
consistent. It should be developed as a regular day-
to-day pattern. It should be reflected in every one
of your supervisory actions and decisions. You cannot change from one policy to another as it suits
your fancy. The moody supervisor is unpredictable.
Each morning employees wonder what he will do
or how he will act. They try to adjust their behavior to his moods. They try to toe the mark but can't
determine what or where the mark is on any particular day.

What are some factors of a healthy working climate? We have already indicated a few in discussing how people are different and how they are alike.
We can now sum up:

1. Make allowance for differences in the way individual employees think, feel, and act.
2. Recognize that all employees —
   a) Want to be part of a group.
   b) Resist change.

    c) Want to feel important and therefore resent criticism.

    d) Desire the approval of others in order to feel secure.

DEVELOPING A HEALTHY CLIMATE

One of the best techniques to help you set up a healthy working climate is the "conference method." Boiled down, this means that you should discuss things with your employees and "let them get into the act." Talk over mutual problems with them. Ask for their suggestions and let them help in making decisions. Explain the reasons for needed changes and get them to agree to them voluntarily. Let them know how they're doing from time to time. Give them recognition, credit, and approval for work well done.

What happens when you try to keep company matters from the workers? It gives them the sense of being "excluded." They get the feeling that things are being done behind their backs. As a result, they are prepared to fight tooth and nail against changes they don't understand. They become extremely sensitive to any form of criticism. Their peace of mind and sense of security are threatened.

A case in point is what took place at an electronics plant when a new executive, a retired army colonel, decided to "tighten up efficiency" by introducing army disciplinary methods. Although the man involved was a top executive, the lesson to be learned can apply to supervisors at all levels.

This former colonel began to issue "Orders of the Day" on special army-style sheets which began

"From: .... To: .... Subject: ...."
He brought in several of his old army aides as his
assistants.

The colonel and his aides mapped plans for increasing production much as they would map a
beach landing — in deepest secrecy. But production, instead of soaring, slumped even more. The
employees became so tense and demoralized that
the company's board of directors was forced to hold
an emergency meeting. Soon afterward, the colonel
was transferred to a job not involving dealings with
plant operations and personnel, and his aides were
fired.

The practice of talking things over with your men
and taking them into your confidence has two advantages: It combines almost all of the principles needed for a healthy company climate which were listed
in a preceding section. It helps develop better solutions to supervisory problems because you are now
drawing on the experience and ideas of many individuals instead of just your own.

What if talking things over doesn't lead to a better solution or improvement? At least you will be
getting the workers to understand the problems and
the necessary action. Follow through and cooperation will develop.

Conducting the Conference

A conference is simply an intelligent discussion of
a problem by two or more interested persons. It is
conducted by a leader, and its purpose is to arrive
at some sort of useful conclusion. There are two
types of conferences. Both involve informal dis-

cussion. One is referred to as a *formal* conference because it takes place in a regular conference room and involves executive or supervisory groups. The second is the *informal* conference. It is the kind you will use most frequently in dealing with your subordinates. The informal conference often takes place right on the job. It may involve anywhere from two to a dozen participants, with you conducting the conference.

A conference, in order to be successful, must stick to the subject at hand. There are four definite points it should cover. Remembering these steps in their proper order will serve as a guide to you, the discussion leader. It will help you keep the conference from getting sidetracked. Or, if this does happen, it will make it easier for you to switch it back to the main line of discussion. The four steps are:

1. *Present the Problem*

The reason nine out of ten conferences bog down is the lack of interest shown by the participants. Your major job is to see that interest is maintained at all times. After calling the conference, make it clear why this particular group was asked to confer at this particular time. Show how the subject concerns the group. Explain why the situation is urgent enough to warrant a discussion *now*. Opening the conference in this way will spark enough interest to get it going successfully. Unless those participating feel a sense of personal interest, they will become bored quickly and contribute little or nothing to the discussion. Next, show what the problem is, thereby providing a jumping-off point for the conference. Present available background and facts.

2. *Explore the Situation*

The workers should now be encouraged to participate in the conference. Let them tell what they know about the situation. Make it plain that whatever facts they can give will help. Ask questions to stimulate discussion. But don't "hog" the spotlight. Don't "lecture" or set yourself up as an expert. Your job should be to make the workers feel you need their assistance.

Sometimes a participant has difficulty making himself understood. He may be confused and nervous. You can help him by offering to clarify his remarks. If he has wandered off the topic, steer him back on. But be diplomatic about it; don't be impatient or impolite. Under no circumstances should you embarrass a member of the group.

What if a worker shows up late for the discussion? Don't ignore him. Interrupt the discussion to brief him quickly on what's been going on. However, don't waste so much time doing it that the others will become bored or lose interest.

3. *Evaluate the Facts*

At this point the discussion is likely to become heated. This is a good sign, in one respect. It indicates that the workers are interested. But don't let the discussion end in a brawl. Remind the participants, if necessary, that the purpose of the conference is to deal with a problem. Keep the discussion going in a constructive channel. Needless disagreements may arise because words or phrases are used that mean different things to different people. Words like "cooperation," "discipline," and "responsibility" can be real troublemakers unless they are

defined clearly so that everyone is talking about the
same thing.

Try to resolve differences of opinion wherever
possible. One way is to show areas of agreement as
well as disagreement between two or more points of
view. Get the group to discuss and weigh the possible effects of each suggested solution on such factors as the individual, the group, and production.

Compliment a participant who makes an especially clear or interesting contribution to the discussion.
But try to balance the discussion. Don't let one or
two individuals monopolize the conference. If participation becomes lopsided, the interest of the others may lag. Try to get everyone to take part. You
might say, for example, "Well, Joe, we haven't heard
from you yet. Do you think we ought to follow
Tom's plan or Mike's? Why?"

Don't be afraid to allow cross-discussion. The
more informal the conference the better the participants will like it and the more effective it will be.
If you have a blackboard available, use it to list important points. Otherwise, a large sheet of paper
will do. Write down possible solutions as they are
suggested so the group can refer back to them.

4. Develop the Final Solution

As conference leader, it is tempting, but unwise,
to "steam-roller" your own opinions. It creates resentment and defeats the very purpose of the conference. Remember that the combined judgment
of the group is more apt to be consistently correct
than the judgment of any one individual.

Whatever final solution or course of action is decided upon by the majority, there may be a minor-

ity who will be unhappy with the decision. It's a good idea for you to explain before the conference breaks up that reaching a democratic decision does not require unanimous opinion. Make it clear that it requires a majority opinion to which the minority must adjust. Remind members of the minority that while they may not be satisfied this time, their ideas may be chosen next time.

Common Mistakes Made by Conference Leaders

In a recent survey of thirty-eight conferences at two large companies, the following were found to be the most common mistakes made by conference leaders:

Failed to gather background and facts about the situation.

Merely sat by taking notes, maintained a dead silence, and failed to take part in conference.

Got off the subject himself or permitted others to do so.

Latecomers were ignored.

Shy members were not encouraged to enter the discussion.

Overtalkative members were not controlled.

Leader constantly referred to his own opinions, made excessive use of phrases like "*I* think" or "*I* feel."

Whispering and side discussions were permitted.

Failed to use exhibits, case histories, charts, and other aids when available.

Spent too much time on details already well-known to the group.

Topic of the conference was not of interest to or the concern of all those present.

Talked too fast, too loud, or mumbled.

Sat or stood in one spot instead of changing position from time to time.

Leader embarrassed participants who made poor presentations.

Failed to compliment speakers who made especially valuable presentations.

"Hogged" the floor, presented material that should have been developed by the participants.

Used dictatorial tone, *telling* instead of asking.

Failed to have group develop conclusions after facts were presented.

Leader "knocked down" opinions differing from his own.

Avoid Objectionable Mannerisms

Your personal mannerisms during the discussion are important. Objectionable mannerisms that distract workers and hinder the conference include:

Drumming on a table, desk, or other objects with fingers or pencil.

Constant staring at ceiling or out a window.

Resting chin in hands with elbows on desk or table.

Conspicuous toying with key chain or similar objects.

Cleaning, examining or biting fingernails.

Rattling keys or coins.

Failing to change facial expression, maintaining frozen smile, etc.

Choose Specific Topics

The more specific the subject of the discussion the more interesting and helpful it will be. For example, a conference dealing with "How Can We Improve Safety Inspections?" is apt to be more valuable than one simply entitled "Safety." Avoid negative topics such as "Why Can't We Get Cooperation With Maintenance People?" A better subject would be "How Can We Cooperate With Maintenance People?"

Preparation Will Help

It's a good idea to prepare questions, charts, diagrams, photographs, exhibits, or models in advance to illustrate the situation under discussion.

DELEGATING RESPONSIBILITY

A major benefit of the conference method is that it gives your subordinates an understanding of what has to be done. It is a democratic way of giving orders and obtaining maximum performance. For a supervisor who is overloaded with duties, it is very helpful. It gives him a chance to delegate many routine tasks to his employees with the knowledge that they will carry them out with a minimum of supervision. It leaves him free to concentrate on more important things.

When assigning duties or responsibilities, there are several important principles to keep in mind:

1. Explain the task thoroughly. Let the employee know its purpose, why it is important, and how it relates to his other work.

2. Get him to describe it back to you so you're certain he understands.

3.   After you're sure he understands, ask him if he feels that he can do it properly.

4.   Agree on a deadline.   In fact it's better to have the employee set the deadline.   There will be no reason for him to complain that you didn't give him enough time.

5.   Tell him you will check with him after he has completed the task.   But let him know *when* you will check.   Then be sure to do so.   Otherwise he'll feel you were just bluffing, and that may lead to problems when you give assignments in the future.

Following these rules will enable you to delegate responsibility more efficiently.   It will improve performance and increase your employees' dependability.   It will cut down the amount of time you'll have to spend supervising routine tasks.   It will give you results instead of alibis and excuses.

EIGHT WAYS TO WIN COOPERATION

COOPERATION MEANS WORKING TOGETHER toward a common goal. Another name for it is teamwork. The picture these terms usually bring to mind is one where everybody pitches in and does his share without grumbling or shirking.

This doesn't tell the whole story. A better way of defining cooperation is that it means going out of your way or inconveniencing yourself to do *more* than your share because you know it will help others or accomplish some over-all good. This is the type of cooperation that is needed to lick the knotty problems and unexpected crises that arise on the job. It is this lofty ideal of teamwork that so often leads the soldier in battle to deeds of heroism "above and beyond the call of duty."

THE VALUE OF COOPERATION ON THE JOB

When a company fails, everybody loses. The employer goes bankrupt, executives lose their jobs, supervisors and workers are laid off, production stops, the public suffers. Thus, it is to everyone's advantage to see that the company succeeds. But this does not always come about when each individual is simply content to do what he's required to do, and no more. The difference between success and failure is often the difference between whether or not employees, supervisors, and executives have adopted an "above and beyond the call of duty" concept of teamwork.

An example of this type of cooperation occurs when a supervisor is willing to limit his own department's output so that he can lend a hand in helping another department break a bottleneck. Though he reduces his own production, his action may be instrumental in increasing the company's over-all output. Such a supervisor shows that he understands the meaning of teamwork in its fullest sense. He sees the work of his department not as an independent operation but as part of a larger production effort.

COOPERATION WITH WHOM?

Many supervisors think of cooperation only in terms of dealings with workers. This is a common mistake. A spirit of teamwork is needed on all levels. It must flow in all directions. In addition to cooperating with your workers, you must cooperate with your fellow supervisors; your superiors; service departments like maintenance, construction, and repair; staff specialists such as time-study and quality-control personnel; and union representatives.

A supervisor may complain that he can't cooperate with other groups because he doesn't know what their problems are. The way to overcome this obstacle is to make it your business to find out something about problems in other departments.

This is not as difficult as it sounds. Part of the answer lies in reading company communications. Most companies today keep their people posted on what is happening within the organization. This is done through conferences, bulletin boards, memos, newsletters, etc. Talk to and compare notes with other supervisors, staff members, and executives. Occasional visits to other departments will help you keep abreast of their problems. Only by "being in the know" and understanding what others are doing can you pave the way for effective cooperation with them.

BARRIERS TO COOPERATION

In recent years there have been a number of surveys to find out why people don't cooperate. In most of these polls the answers of persons questioned — whether they were workers, supervisors, or executives — have been strikingly similar. Following is a list of the most frequent reasons given for noncooperation:

Fear — *"I'm not sticking my neck out to help him."*

Jealousy — *"We are both bucking for the same promotion. Let him do it himself."*

Antagonism — *"After what he did to me last week, I'm not going to help him."*

Misunderstanding — *"I didn't realize that this would help the other boys."*

You have only to glance at this list to realize that the faults mentioned are human ones. You probably have seen them in the people around you. They are real obstacles to cooperation.

There is still another barrier to teamwork. This is the tendency to expect cooperation before giving it. It is a cause of noncooperation that rarely occurs to us, yet it is a fault that is almost universal. It is probably the biggest obstacle of all to effective teamwork.

For example, when asked to give what we feel are reasons for lack of cooperation, what are some of our answers? They take this form: "The other supervisor won't cooperate because he is afraid someone will steal his thunder." Or, "If the production foremen weren't so jealous of us white-collar people, they'd be more cooperative."

We take the attitude that it is not *we* who have these faults; it is always the other fellow. It's never *we* who refuse to cooperate, it's the fellow at the next machine, the next desk, or in the next department.

The "Unofficial Leader"

As mentioned earlier, you must be something of a psychologist. If you are an observer of human nature, you will soon recognize that people who work together tend to break up into groups or "cliques." These groups are formed because each member has something in common with the other members: it may be age, background, skills, hobbies, or any one of a dozen things. You will also discover that in every group there is always one individual who, because of his personality, has more influence over the group than any other member. This person, whether man or woman, is its informal leader — a sort of "unofficial supervisor." Because he has leadership influence over the group, this "unofficial supervisor" does not want to be treated as just another worker.

The informal leader has no official status. An inexperienced or inept supervisor may be tempted to ignore him. He may resent the "unofficial supervisor's" influence over the rest of the workers and even show open hostility to him. There is always a danger, however, that the informal leader will use his weight to turn the group against him.

The wise supervisor avoids such a situation. Instead of competing for authority with the informal leader, he uses him as a key to handling the rest of the workers. He learns how to get along with him. He shows the employees that he recognizes and respects their informal leader. When a change in policy or other matter comes up that the supervisor wants his men to accept, he first takes it up with the informal leader. Once he has won over the "unofficial supervisor," he uses the prestige and influence of this leader to help win the others.

The successful supervisor also makes it clear to his men that he will not hesitate to share his knowledge with them and will not withhold credit or praise to which they may be entitled. He avoids giving the impression that he will stand in the way of their advancement. He knows that by helping an employee under him to succeed, he automatically raises his own status in the eyes of top management and places himself in line for greater responsibility. He trains a capable worker to replace him. In this way he not only is covered during vacation, sick leave, or other absences, but he is free for promotion when an opening is available.

COOPERATION MUST BE GIVEN BEFORE IT CAN BE RECEIVED

You cannot get cooperation by demanding it. Nor does it help to sit back and complain about the lack of it. If you're not getting cooperation, step back and examine yourself. Is it really the other fellow who is not cooperating? Or are you at fault?

The real secret of winning cooperation is to give it first. And you must continue giving it without expecting immediate returns on your investment. It's like priming a pump. Even when the well is full, you may have to pump the handle several times before water flows. Eventually your efforts will be rewarded.

You may have to help someone two, three, or four times before the opportunity for him to repay you arises. It's a human trait to want to repay kindness in kind.

EIGHT WAYS TO WIN COOPERATION

Your success in winning cooperation depends to a great extent on your ability to deal with people. Here, as in other functions of your supervisory job, there are definite skills you should develop. By learning to apply these skills properly, you can create a spirit of effective teamwork with those who work with you, whether they are subordinates, fellow supervisors, or superiors.

1. *Avoid Arguments*

Perhaps you'll say this is easier said than done. What happens, you may ask, if someone comes running up to you red-faced and indignant about some real or imagined injustice? Skillful handling can usually avert an argument that might lead to serious trouble.

Never walk away or try to shut the person up. Since he is already steaming, this would merely increase the pressure within him to the boiling point. Let him tell his story without interruption. When he's finished, allow a few seconds more for him to recall details he may have overlooked, or to repeat the more aggravating parts of his complaint. A sympathetic and understanding ear is the most useful safety valve for warding off a potential explosion.

Next, arrange for a further cooling-off period. Suggest that you'd like to look into the problem further, think it over, or discuss a solution later on. Even if you have the answer now, hold on to it. If it's morning, suggest a second meeting in the afternoon. If it's the afternoon, put the matter off until the following morning. There is good reason for this. Since the person is still tense and excited, he isn't likely to listen to an explanation, no matter how logical. Emotional problems rarely are solved by presenting facts or a book of rules. When you are ready and equipped with a full estimate of the situation, give your opinion about the matter. Don't criticize. Don't try to prove the other person factually wrong. It makes him feel stupid and embarrassed. You may win the immediate skirmish, but the long-range aim of building cooperation is lost.

Try to agree with points in the other person's favor. Arguments thrive on opposition and die on agreement. You can usually find something in the other person's side of the story to agree with. It is rare for one individual to be completely right and the other completely wrong. Once you've established points of agreement, "lead" the person along so that he will come of his own accord to the answer you had in mind. You enable him to save face and credit himself with reaching the right conclusion.

Remember that every heated argument has two losers and no winners. Each person is too busy thinking how to prove his own case to be convinced of the merits of the opposing point of view. He'll wait — or interrupt — impatiently to present his own side without really listening to you. In the end he'll walk away a little bit angrier and more convinced than ever that he is right.

2. *Admit Your Errors*

The best policy is to avoid making mistakes in the first place. But there are times when all of us commit blunders. We have a choice of trying to cover up our errors or admitting to them frankly.

Covering up mistakes requires that you hide them, lie about them, or pass off the blame to someone else. It often leads to repetition of the error. In the long run it fools no one since the truth is bound to come out eventually. Covering up mistakes creates resentment and gossip. You lose stature in the eyes of your men. Most people dislike the person who is "always right," especially if he tries to give that impression even when he and they both know he's wrong.

No one has ever lost the respect of his fellows by honestly admitting to a mistake. Just the opposite is true. It pictures you in the eyes of others as a human being. It inspires the added confidence of your subordinates, fellow supervisors, and superiors. It also sets an example for employees so that they won't hesitate to come to you when they are in error. At the same time, a frank admission helps impress the mistake on your own mind so that you're less likely to repeat it in the future.

3. *Establish a Receptive Frame of Mind*

The human mind operates in such a way that effort is required for it to change from agreement to disagreement and vice versa. Once you have a person in a "Yes" frame of mind, it becomes difficult for him to say "No." You may recall an old word game based on this principle. Ask someone how he pronounces the letters j-o-k-e, and he immediately says, "Joke." Next, ask him the name of the heavy wooden collar used for a team of oxen. He replies, "Yoke." Now, you ask for a word meaning the white of an egg. In almost every case, the response is "Yolk." The correct answer, of course, is "albumen," since it is the yellow part that is the yolk.

This principle of establishing a receptive frame of mind is well known by salesmen and advertising writers. Take the case of a door-to-door salesman who is out to sell your wife an encyclopedia. If he knows his business at all, he'd never think of simply asking, "Would you like to buy this encyclopedia?" Instead, he will probably knock at the door, excuse himself for taking up your wife's time, and ask politely, "Do you have any children?"

If the answer is "Yes," he follows it up with another question: "Do they ever ask you any questions?"

This time the reply is likely to be a hearty, interested one: "Well of course they do! They pester me with all kinds of questions."

The salesman now produces his sample book, opens it, and says, "This book has pictures and the answers to all their questions. Would you like to own a copy?"

The salesman, by his questions, seeks to establish a receptive frame of mind. After two or three "Yes" answers it becomes hard for the prospective customer to say "No."

In a sense, too, this is what the advertising writer does when he prepares an advertisement showing a pretty girl wearing the "x" brand of garment or smoking the "y" brand of cigarette. The girl serves as an "eye catcher." The advertising writer attempts to set up a receptive frame of mind. He hopes that the admiration of the men and the desire of women readers to be like the girl in the ad will be transferred to the product he is selling.

Does this mean you must lure people into doing what you want them to do? Not at all. Most of us, even when we are in favor of something, are reluctant to put forth the effort required to move from the "thinking about it" phase to the active or "doing it" stage. Usually it is only when we have been made to feel a keen personal concern because we, our families, or other members of our immediate group are involved, that we are moved to action.

You have merely to look around you to see examples of this. For instance, almost every citizen will tell you he's in favor of good government. With one or two exceptions, however, when Election Day rolls around, less than half of those Americans eligible to vote take the trouble to go to the polls.

To a certain extent the same is true of cooperation on the job. The people you work with are basically of a cooperative nature. But they have to be led to the "action" stage. In order to do this you must establish a receptive frame of mind.

You can put people in a "Yes" mood by getting them to "agree" before asking them to "buy" your decision. Get them to agree that something must be done. Let them see for themselves how the group as a whole — and they as individual members — will benefit. Finally, get them to agree that their active cooperation is essential.

Assume you are an office manager who has just noticed that the room where office supplies are stored is badly in need of reorganization. This is a tedious, undesirable job. How should you approach the woman employee whom you have in mind for the task?

One way would be to go up to her and simply order her to do it. Her reaction might be, "Why pick on me?" You would probably get the job done, but chances are it would be carried out carelessly and with a lot of grumbling.

A better approach would be first to get her to agree that a reorganization is necessary. Find out if she and her fellow-employees are having trouble locating the supplies they need. Get her ideas on how the job should be done. Ask her if she really thinks the new system will improve the situation. Having agreed on the need for the reorganization, the new system to be used, and the fact that it will make things easier for her and her fellow-employees, it will be hard for her to say "No" when you finally suggest that she undertake the job. And, since you've established a receptive frame of mind, you can be sure she'll carry out the task with far more care than if you had simply ordered her to do it.

4. A Sympathetic "No" Is Better than a Harsh "Yes"

We've stressed the importance of finding areas of agreement in order to resolve differences and avoid arguments. This doesn't mean that you must seek to agree at any price. A wishy-washy supervisor is never a good leader. Like the too-harsh boss, he soon loses the respect of his subordinates, fellow supervisors, and superiors.

Situations often arise where "No" is the only answer. You may be forced to disagree on the merits of a particular idea, or suggestion, turn down an employee's request for some favor, or reject an unsatisfactory excuse. Unfortunately, no one has yet found a way to say "No" so that it is entirely satisfactory to the person or persons involved. But with a little planning and effort you can usually minimize the disappointment and resentment it is bound to cause.

How can you disagree with or refuse someone and yet keep the doors open to future cooperation? The answer lies in doing it without wounding the individual's pride, dignity, or ego. Here are some of the things to keep in mind when saying "No":

a) Be friendly. Put the other person at his ease.

b) Listen patiently. Hear the full story. Take a real interest in what he has to say.

c) Where you honestly agree with certain points he's made, let him know you think he's right.

d) Explain thoroughly your reasons for saying "No" at this time, to this request.

e) Be as tactful as possible. Although you've been forced to turn him down, there is no reason to make him lose face in the process.

f) Let him know your door is always open to him. Indicate that he's welcome to return with any future grievances, problems, suggestions, or requests.

g) End on an appreciative note. Thank him for coming to you. If you can sincerely compliment him on his past work, it's a good idea to do so at this point. The word "No" is always less bitter when it is sweetened with a bit of merited praise.

5. *Dramatize Ideas or Suggestions*

To get a person to cooperate on a particular project, you must first get him to agree on its value. Sell him on the merit of the idea. The best way to do this is to dramatize it wherever possible.

We often try to explain ideas merely by "telling" them. Since many people have trouble translating what they hear into a clear mental picture, this can lead to unnecessary misunderstanding and disagreement.

The sense of sight is the strongest and most useful of our five senses. Most of what we learn is absorbed through the eyes. When dramatizing ideas, therefore, it's wise to make use of visual aids when you can. Visual aids include charts, photos, demonstrations, drawings, films, etc. They help you utilize the other person's most efficient organ of learning.

6. *Set a Fair Challenge*

People like to rise to challenges. They respond readily when an appeal is made to their ability or pride of workmanship. You do, yourself. Suppose a rush job comes up and your boss advises you that you and your men will have to stay late for three nights to get it finished. You will probably grumble and feel sorry for yourself. But suppose your boss says, "We have an important job here that we have to get out by Thursday noon. I'm going to turn it over to you. Will you see if you can get it done in time?" With such a challenge, you will probably throw yourself into the job enthusiastically and work as late as necessary to do a first-rate job.

When flatly ordered to perform a difficult task, most of us tend to throw up our hands in the air.

But when a job is presented in such a way as to arouse our competitive spirit, the picture changes. We perform better and are more cooperative when we are presented with a challenging goal. Incentive pay systems use this principle. So does the practice of posting production records where everyone can see them.

People like to make comparisons with their own earlier records and try to beat them. Letting employees know how they're doing is a dependable everyday incentive.

To be effective, a challenge must be fair; it must be attainable. This doesn't mean it should be easy. Overcoming obstacles gives people an opportunity for self-expression and personal accomplishment. They like to meet a production standard that seems almost beyond reach, eliminate a difficulty in some phase of work, or complete a job under unusual working conditions. But a job that is so tough as to be completely beyond a person's ability will quickly kill his self-confidence and interest.

The best challenges are short-range ones. To the average person, winning five dollars next week is more important than winning ten dollars a year from now. If a job is long and involved, it's good psychology to divide it up into a number of short-range goals instead of a single one at the end. As soon as one objective is passed, the men and women you work with can set their sights on the next goal.

7. *Praise in Advance*

Many old-line supervisors contend that the business of dispensing praise is nonsense. Give a man a pat on the back, they say, and he will hit you for a raise the next day. It does not work out that way. Employees in modern business and industry are realistic. They understand that the company, from the supervisor up to the top boss himself, is bound by budgets and pay schedules. They understand that most wages are set by labor agreements.

You might also hear that if you start treating people nicely, they will walk all over you. Ask yourself, "If someone is nice to me, do I try to walk all over him?" The answer is "No." It's important to keep in mind that the people you work with — employees, fellow supervisors, and superiors — are human. If they are treated as important persons, they will respond every time by cooperating with you.

We pointed out in the previous chapter that people need appreciation. They feel a deep hunger for praise. It gives them a sense of personal achievement. Even the worst grouch secretly yearns for a little honest recognition. A wise supervisor is able to find something to commend in even the least competent man or women who works with him.

You can also get more cooperation by praising in advance. People have a tendency to do what is expected of them. If they are treated as if they can't do much, they don't try very hard. When they realize that you expect a great deal of them, they will try to live up to your expectations by putting forth their best efforts. For example, if you want the cooperation of a fellow supervisor, you might say, "Bill, you've been around longer than I; you know more about this job than I do. I'm having a little trouble and I wonder if you can help me iron it out?" When you put it that way, Bill will do his best.

8. *Don't Demand Cooperation*

You cannot force people to cooperate. True co-operation can only come on a voluntary basis. If you need help, particularly if it calls for someone to go out of his way or inconvenience himself, ask for it. Don't order or demand it. People enjoy helping when the decision to cooperate is theirs. They resent being forced to do so.

Most people possess far greater physical and mental ability than they normally use. Some authorities claim the average person draws upon only one-half of his potential ability. We are like high-powered automobiles crawling along at twenty-five miles an hour on a superhighway built for speeds of fifty or sixty.

When do we tap this reservoir of unused power? How do we release the brakes? This is done only when we're so interested and get so much satisfaction in what we're doing that we have the will to unleash the power. The desire must come from within us. We cannot be made to do so.

Here is a brief story that might illustrate the point. It happened at a large oil refinery several years ago. A member of the company baseball team had been switched to the night shift. The morning before a game with a rival company, he was out on the ball-field practicing with his teammates. Spotting him, the team manager came over and asked, "What are you doing here? I thought you worked last night."

"Sure I did," he replied. "But it's my turn to pitch."

When you succeed in winning a person's coopera-tion, you know that he's helping because he *wants* to — because he gets satisfaction from doing so. He will always give more of himself than if he were simply ordered to cooperate. Developing cooperation is a key to unlocking the valuable storehouse of unused human energy that is present in most people.

When asking for cooperation, a direct request may not even be necessary. A mere hint or suggestion may be enough to awaken the individual's helpful impulse. Let him decide whenever possible how to help you and how much to do. In this way he feels that the idea to cooperate originated with him. He also feels that he had a say in how the task should be done. He has a dual personal interest in seeing it turn out successfully.

CHECK LIST

Eight Ways To Win Cooperation

1. Avoid arguments.

2. Be frank in admitting your errors.

3. Establish a receptive frame of mind by getting "group think" decisions before putting them into effect.

4. Learn to say "No" sympathetically.

5. Dramatize what has to be done so others will understand it.

6. Set up challenges to develop enthusiasm.

7. Praise people in advance so they will try to live up to your expectations.

8. Ask for help instead of demanding it.

FIVE WAYS TO IMPROVE MORALE

MORALE IS THE CLIMATE OR ATMOSPHERE prevailing in a company. It is always present. It involves a group spirit — a feeling of good will among employees working together. It determines whether they are willing to work with each other toward a common goal. It determines whether an organization is successful.

Good morale doesn't mean that everybody must agree 100 per cent on all issues. It requires healthy job attitudes so differences can be ironed out smoothly and without injury to the company's operation. As someone once said: "If two men on the same job agree all the time, one of them is useless. If they never agree, both are useless."

Poor morale shows up in high absenteeism and high turnover rates, waste, high accident frequency, widespread griping, or complete absence of grievances. It is no exaggeration to say that millions of employees throughout the nation are working with their brakes on because of poor company atmosphere or morale.

Morale cannot be isolated from the problems of discipline, cooperation, safety, job methods, and the other factors discussed in this book. It is the product of all of these. In this chapter, however, we will examine some special factors that affect morale.

Good morale usually stems from the top. With management support, the supervisor can do much to create favorable on-the-job attitudes and improve employee morale. Yet it is surprising in how many plants the bottleneck is found at the top of the bottle, where the "cream" is supposed to be. While the individual supervisor can do little to change such an over-all condition, he has the power within his own department of making the best of even a bad company situation.

Surveys have shown that employees will double their output or usefulness if given good leadership by their immediate supervisors. A research organization recently investigated the effect of good and bad supervision by going into a corporation where several departments had practically identical working conditions, except for the quality of supervision. The pay, kind of work, and surroundings were the same in these departments. The researchers compared the department having the "best" production record with the department having the "worst." In the best department almost every employee spoke highly of his immediate supervisor; in the worst department, only 26 per cent spoke well of him.

Another survey of 20,000 employees at a large automotive plant indicates some of the symptoms that accompany a condition of low company morale. Here are a few of the findings:

Eighteen per cent of the employees felt it would be actually "dangerous" for them to express their honest opinions to their bosses.

Seventy per cent felt that their bosses were making little or no effort to make them feel they were a part of the company.

Forty-three per cent felt they had little real chance to talk over their work or ideas with their supervisors.

Such findings clearly show that morale is not determined by wages alone. A labor leader of a transport union in one of the world's largest cities pointed out that of twenty-four labor flare-ups on the city's bus lines in a single year, fewer than half were about money.

It would be a mistake to say that morale is not affected at all by factors like pay, job security, pension plans, and length of vacations. These things do influence company morale. Yet experience shows that some organizations offering the best working conditions suffer from constant absenteeism, tardiness, labor turnover, poor production, and other troubles associated with poor morale.

Some of the basic factors affecting morale include:

1. The employee's pride in his work and sense of satisfaction in doing a good job.
2. His attitude toward his boss.
3. His ambition to get ahead.
4. His feeling of being treated fairly.
5. His ability to get along with his co-workers.
6. His awareness of his job's responsibility.

In any type of employment these are factors that come into play every working day. We can say, therefore, that good morale involves an over-all job satisfaction which results from the sum total of "little" everyday satisfactions. You can help to provide these daily satisfactions. You prove to your men that you respect them as human beings instead of as so many units of muscle power. You also show them that you recognize that the *spirit* of the group working together is the keystone of any organized work activity which combines men, materials, and equipment.

Here are five clear-cut actions you can take to maintain high morale among the people under your supervision:

1. *Let Each Worker Know How He's Getting Along*

Every employee wants to know where he stands. If he's doing good work, he likes to feel that it is noticed and appreciated. If his work is unsatisfactory, he should be told so he can do something about it. Keeping workers posted on how well or how badly they are doing accomplishes this goal. The alert supervisor uses every honest opportunity to let his men know what the score is. He gives recognition to the employee who is doing better-than-average work. Below-average performance is also recognized and discussed. But the supervisor takes care to focus criticism where it belongs: on the work, not on the worker as an individual. He avoids personalizing his constructive suggestions.

Whenever any employee does work below satisfactory standards, the good supervisor will give him help, not hell. He knows that nothing is achieved by riding a man into a jittery state and thereby making him fail.

Many companies have a formal way of letting workers know how they are doing through "merit rating systems." These are also known as "performance reviews." The Federal Civil Service has such a rating system. Periodically, supervisors are called on to fill out forms rating each subordinate on job knowledge, dependability, attitude, output, attendance, and other factors.

Other companies use specific factors that are important in the particular job of the worker who is being rated. If the employee is a salesperson, how he rates on "customer relations" may be important. A receptionist might be judged on "personal appearance." A secretary who is required to perform a variety of different duties would very likely be rated on "adaptability."

A common procedure is for the supervisor, after completing the rating form, to go over it with his superior. Next, he reviews it with the employee involved. He compliments him on the good work he is doing. If the form indicates weaknesses, the supervisor and worker together try to find out the reasons why. The supervisor may offer help or advice on how the employee can bring his next rating up to the "satisfactory" mark.

A "performance review" can be very constructive in guiding and developing your subordinates. But its success depends almost entirely on you. For supervisors with a desire to be well-liked and "popular with the boys," there is a strong temptation to give high ratings even when they are not deserved. As a result, neither top management nor the worker are aware of weak spots. If the employee eventually develops into a real problem, and suspension, dismissal, or demotion is in order, the supervisor may be in a real dilemma. He'll find it hard to justify such action in the face of the high ratings he has given the same employee in the past.

In large organizations where performance reviews are company-wide policy, uniformity requires the use of printed or mimeographed forms. This formal type of merit rating system serves two good purposes: It is a way of letting the worker know where he stands, and it offers the supervisor an opportunity to give his subordinates credit or help. The forms also serve as a permanent personnel record to be referred to when the question of promotions, raises, transfers and layoffs come up.

Even in organizations where there are no merit rating systems, each supervisor has it within his authority to informally institute such a plan in his own department.

If you have a large group of employees under your supervision, you will find that preparing your own merit rating sheet or marking down your ratings in a notebook will help you keep an accurate record on each person. The ratings can be made monthly, quarterly, or semiannually, depending on the type of work and the amount of time you can devote to the task.

But whether you follow a formal or an informal system, make it your business to interview every worker on a regular basis to talk about his progress.

When discussing an employee's shortcomings, it is always a good policy first to mention the things he does well. By creating a friendly atmosphere, you will find him more receptive to your suggestions and advice on how he can improve.

2. *Tell Employees in Advance about Changes that Will Affect Them*

One of the most effective ways of destroying morale is to make a sudden change affecting employees without first preparing them thoroughly by showing it is a wise or necessary move. Most people don't like to have things sprung on them. Yet some companies notify employees at the last minute that work-ing hours have been moved up, payday has been changed from Thursday to Friday, or working locations have been changed from Building A to Building B. Abrupt changes are upsetting; they don't give employees time to adjust. Even where a change will benefit them, they get a feeling that they are being pushed around. They assume the supervisor and top management have no considera-tion for their feelings; they feel that they are just cogs in a machine. In a survey at one large com-pany, 53 per cent of the employees complained they didn't get enough information about what was hap-pening in the company.

Failing to prepare workers for abrupt changes can lead to serious problems. At an eastern steel mill absenteeism among cranemen suddenly became a big issue. In spite of the efforts of management to solve the problem, the cranemen soon went out on strike. They complained that the air around their crane cabs was filled with irritating fumes. They refused to return to work until an expensive — and unnecessary — ventilating system was installed.

What was really bothering these men was their new supervisor. He was a former craneman him-self. He knew from his own experience that many improvements could be made in operating methods, and he began to introduce them all at once. The changes came so fast and abruptly that his subordi-nates, all old-timers on the job, became confused. Their sense of security was disturbed and they felt resentful without knowing exactly why. When the men returned to work after the new ventilating sys-tem was installed, they found other things to complain about. The new supervisor grasped the real problem. He began to consult his group before introducing changes and the men began to work with him instead of against him. Talking about a change did much to overcome resistance.

At a metal-container company a highly-paid designer came to his office one day and found a stranger sitting behind his desk. A secretary handed him a note from the boss asking him to sit at a desk out in the anteroom for a few days. The designer became sullen and snappish. He felt humiliated, and the quality of his work deteriorated. He was restored to his office ten days later, just as abruptly. There had been a temporary dislocation while the company's executive offices on another floor were being redecorated. The boss had assumed the designer would understand without a detailed explanation why someone else had moved into his office. He didn't.

Keep your men posted on all matters that affect them as workers. Let them know in advance about such things as a change in location or layout, introduction of new production methods, reallotment of office space, or payroll-procedure changes. If the change is to be a major one, it should be introduced gradually. Whenever possible, give your men the reasons why a change has to be made. Never assume that employees will understand without being told why a change has been decided upon, no matter how logical the change may seem. Giving them plenty of advance notice and telling them why something new will have to be added is a good way of reducing employees' resentment and misunderstanding.

3. *Make the Best Use of Each Person's Ability*

Since job interest is a critical factor in employee morale, each worker should be assigned wherever possible to the work that he likes to do and does best. More and more companies are screening and testing new employees before assigning them to jobs. In companies that do not have a formal placement program, the all-important matter of work assignments is left to the discretion of the supervisor.

A progressive supervisor will take the time and trouble to study the worker's background and experience. When possible, within the limits of his department, he will try to assign the employee to work that is both challenging to him and within his capabilities.

A job that isn't interesting or challenging becomes monotonous. Monotony produces fatigue. One study in a large transportation company revealed that bus operators with the highest intelligence ratings also had the highest accident rate. A university survey showed that the safest automobile drivers are those of below average intelligence.

A supervisor who tries to balance his employees' abilities and interests when making work assignments will discover that it pays off in safety, high production, quality, and output, low labor turnover and absenteeism, and other dividends commonly associated with good employee morale.

4. *Make Assignments and Enforce Rules Fairly*

Workers don't mind doing what they have to do. But they are concerned with what they have to do as compared with what the fellow at the next desk or machine has to do. People will always rise to fair challenges. They will accept difficult situations if they know others are carrying their fair share of the burden. This is particularly true of salary. A stenographer in New York isn't bothered by the fact that a stenographer in Los Angeles is receiving ten dollars a week more. But she is concerned about what the girl in the next department is getting.

The worker who knows that his supervisor has a "dirty" job for him doesn't mind doing it if he knows it's his turn in a fair rotation. But he resents being "stuck" with it again and again. One of the most common complaints of employees is: "What's the use of trying hard with Joe as foreman? He has his favorite boys and they get all the breaks."

Actually, avoiding favoritism is harder than it sounds. A supervisor may honestly feel he isn't showing partiality, yet he may be guilty of unintentional or accidental favoritism. The reason for this is that every individual has his personal likes and dislikes. We may like one person because he lives in our neighborhood, belongs to the same lodge, or likes the same hobbies we do; we may dislike another because of the color of his hair, tone of his voice, physical appearance, or the friends he keeps. We do not even realize that these prejudices are part of us. They show themselves in ways we are not aware of and at times when we least expect them. It is easy to understand, therefore, how a supervisor can favor one employee over another without even knowing that he is being partial.

How can you avoid partiality, real or imagined? The fairest and most workable solution is to "keep score." Try to rotate the dirty jobs. Spread the "good breaks" so that everyone has a chance at them.

Post assignment sheets on the bulletin board showing how the rotation system works. Keep a written record available so that employees can refer to it. Everyone can see for himself when his turn will come up and knows that the supervisor is playing "fair and square."

Many companies follow a policy of keeping written records when it comes to vacation schedules and opportunities for overtime pay. You may find it helpful to extend the following idea, as one supervisor in a blouse factory did recently:

The company employed its sewing machine operators on a piecework basis. Each time an operator was given a batch of "large sizes" she felt she was being "stuck" and complained about losing pay. To eliminate complaints the supervisor began keeping a written record to assure herself that the large- and small-size batches were being assigned fairly. Yet the complaints continued. She hit on the idea of taping the record to the side of her desk where everybody could see and refer to it. The complaints vanished immediately.

A supervisor may seem to show favoritism by assigning the same employee time and again to a job the others consider easy or especially desirable. The reason may be that the employee is the only qualified person for that job. Other employees, not understanding this, become angry and resentful.

What if the desirable job requires a special skill making it impossible to use a rotation plan? Explain this carefully to your men before making the assignment. You can say, for example, "Now I know all of you would like a crack at this job. And I'd like to give you a chance. But it seems John has the best experience and training to fill it. However, if any of you feel you have qualifications for the job that I don't know about, I'll be glad to talk them over with you."

Employee morale also depends on how company rules are enforced. If a regulation is to be enforced at all, it should be done fairly. Making an exception without reason or explanation exposes the supervisor to charges of preferential treatment, even when he doesn't mean to play favorites. A worker who punches in late may not mind having the supervisor demand an explanation. But he is resentful and feels he is being "picked on" if he knows that not a word was said to Johnny Smith who was late the day before.

5. *Resist the Temptation to Throw Your Weight Around*

Power can be a dangerous thing. The more power a man has, the more he is tempted to use it, because it seems the simplest and quickest way to accomplish what he wants. In the long run, this "BIG ME and little you" attitude destroys good morale. Tactlessly criticizing or "bawling out" an employee humiliates him. You cannot get the best work out of a person if you ruffle his vanity. Tongue-lashings do more to distract workers from successful performance of their duties than almost any other factor.

In addition, a supervisor who allows himself to become involved in an argument with a subordinate is helping to lower morale. As pointed out in the previous chapter, it is next to impossible to argue anyone around to your point of view. The other person is usually so busy trying to defend himself and save face that he isn't even listening to you. A supervisor who triumphantly hauls out a company manual to prove to a worker that he is wrong loses the employee's good will.

Some supervisors throw their weight around in another way. They use subordinates to do personal chores for them. Most employees resent the boss who habitually asks them to do such jobs. They feel he is taking unfair advantage of his position. No matter what their job classification, they don't like the feeling of inferiority that goes with being treated as an "errand boy." It sets a bad example. They conclude that they, too, are entitled to use company time for personal business. One-sided favors, when demanded again and again, seriously hamper good morale.

The supervisor can better follow the actions suggested in this chapter if he:

a) Knows the individual characteristics of his employees.

b) Uses regular channels of communication.

c) Gives special consideration to new workers.

Know Your Types

While all people respond better if they are given feelings of security and recognition, some incentives are more effective than others. The supervisor who wants to develop good worker morale should try to figure out what each of his employees seems to want first — praise, security, promotion, money, etc. He will soon get to know his types. He'll recognize, for example, that the quiet, shy employee needs frequent pats on the back; that he respects a supervisor who will help him feel at ease with his co-workers and will protect him from the horseplay and practical jokes of the overexuberant employees. The loud, happy-go-lucky employee, on the other hand, doesn't need pats as much as he needs a stage where he can show off. He may be fine at running a plant contest or handing out parts in a supply room where he can come in contact with lots of people and keep up a running chatter. Tie him down to a machine, however, and he may become disgruntled.

The supervisor who knows his types will also be able to gauge just how much supervision his workers need in order to maintain good morale. If he is in New England, for example, he might take into account the fact that skilled Yankee workmen tend to be stubbornly independent and like to take responsibility for working out their own jobs. If he is in a highly industrialized and populated city like New York or Chicago, he should realize that employees there are more dependent. Usually they have no homes or gardens of their own and feel less secure. The city dwellers do not have the social reinforcement of the small town. They appreciate close, sympathetic supervision. On the other hand, a supervisor in a West Virginia plant, where labor is drawn mainly from the hills, should know that employees need close watching but must be handled with kid gloves or they will take off for their farms.

THE "CHAIN-OF-COMMAND" PROBLEM

To operate efficiently, a company must have a regular channel of authority that is adhered to by workers, supervisors, and administrators. In the

Army and Navy this is called the "chain of command." Unless it is adhered to, organized activity is likely to break down. Company directives, communications between employees and management, and the issuance of orders should be done *through* and not *around* each link in the chain of command.

A certain amount of flexibility must be tolerated if good morale is to prevail. It would be ridiculous for a department head, when asked what time it is by a worker, to reply, "See your supervisor." Similarly, in emergency situations, especially when danger is present, the line of authority may have to be bypassed temporarily.

Almost every employee soon learns that he must respect the chain of command. He realizes that if he wishes to see the department head or personnel manager, the accepted procedure is to inform his supervisor first. In turn, the supervisor, interested in maintaining high employee morale, will not stop the worker. He will not set himself up as a dictator or final authority. He lets his people know that they can always appeal to higher authority through him if they feel they have been treated unfairly. If he senses that they are hesitant or afraid to do so, he will even encourage them.

Occasionally the supervisor's real problem is not how to get his men to respect the chain of command, but how to get higher management to adhere to it. Many violations are from the top down, not from the bottom up. A department head or other executive who sees a worker doing something that he considers wrong is understandably anxious to set things straight. Without first talking to the supervisor, he issues conflicting orders. He may not stop to think that there may be special circumstances or conditions which require a job to be done differently from the way he believes best. It may not occur to him that his impulsiveness will undermine the supervisor's authority. Another morale destroyer is created when two representatives of management disagree in front of employees.

MORALE AND THE NEW EMPLOYEE

How a supervisor breaks in a new worker is important in determining the employee's attitude toward his job. The steps in training new people are discussed in detail in a later chapter. Yet in any mention of employee morale, it should be emphasized that a person trying to adjust to a new job or a new company goes through some hectic moments. You should realize, for example, that a newcomer may not want to ask questions for fear of appearing stupid. Give him special attention and consideration. Give him a friendly welcome, guide him around the offices or plant, and explain the whole operation. Make him feel right at home. A large baking organization trained its supervisors in this friendly approach and reduced the normal breaking-in and training phase from six to less than three weeks.

CHECK LIST

Five Ways To Improve Morale

1. Let each worker employee know how he's getting along.

2. Tell employees in advance about changes that will affect them.

3. Make the best use of each employee's ability.

4. Make assignments and enforce rules on a fair basis.

5. Don't throw your weight around.

DISCIPLINE

A SUPERVISOR'S DUTIES include controlling production results such as quality, quantity, cost, and safety. The results he gets depend on *conditions in the working area* and *employee performance.*

Controlling the worker's performance is by far the more difficult job. A bad condition can almost always be remedied. When a machine breaks down it can usually be repaired to operate properly for some time. If a loose pipe is left lying in an aisle where it is a safety hazard, it can be removed. But the employee who is in the habit of reporting late or disturbing other employees by being loud and boisterous offers a more difficult problem.

You may not notice the worker committing the violation the first time. He may break the same rule or repeat the same error several times before you catch up with him. Even if you do correct him, he may soon forget or simply ignore the correction the moment you turn your back.

Controlling employee performance comes under the heading of "discipline." Most of us think of discipline largely in terms of imposing penalties or punishment. Actually, punishing the worker is but one aspect of the general problem of discipline. It enters the picture only in the minority of cases where all constructive approaches have failed.

In its most useful form, discipline is a force that develops within the worker himself and causes him to conform on a voluntary basis to rules, regulations, and high standards of work and behavior.

Discipline is derived from the word "disciple," meaning "a follower." It stands to reason that if there are to be followers, a leader is needed. You are the leader and the workers under your supervision are your followers. In order to get good discipline, you must provide good leadership.

The importance of effective leadership cannot be overemphasized. A poor leader who throws his weight around and uses constant threats can sometimes obtain what appears to be good discipline. The workers follow company rules to the letter and seem to be doing their jobs without grumbling. But outward appearances can be deceiving. They may merely be a "cover-up" to hide a powder keg of resentment and ill-feeling.

Obedience through fear should not be confused with effective discipline. Threats and force may serve for a time. But the hidden unrest and insecurity that result from strict regimentation and the use of force alone are liable to explode in the supervisor's face at any moment.

How can we gauge good discipline? In general, proper discipline prevails when employees come to work regularly and on time; when they are dressed properly for their jobs; when they handle materials and equipment with care; when they turn out a satisfactory amount of quality work and follow the job methods set up by the company; and when they do their work in good spirits. These standards must be maintained on a daily basis. And since anything done on a regular basis soon becomes a habit, we can say that people trained in good habits are well-disciplined.

Employees are never born with good or bad working habits. They develop them on the job. Thus you have a direct influence on the type of habits your men develop. They are established by you through the supervisory climate in your department as well as by the personal example you set. The specific methods you use in developing good working habits among your subordinates should vary according to the particular situation and employee involved. For example, your methods may range from a simple observation or comment to correcting, reinstructing, reminding, encouraging, repeating, admonishing, warning, and, in some cases, penalizing.

Most people will respond to good leadership by developing desirable working habits. Some may require special attention. And there are always a few who will have to be dealt with more sternly. As you develop leadership know-how and experience, you soon learn which techniques are called for in specific instances.

How Habits Develop

A habit is any action, way of thinking, or way of feeling that is repeated many times by an individual and gives him a sense of satisfaction. The first time the action occurs, it happens because the person *decided* to do it. He may have made a snap decision or given it a good deal of thought beforehand. But the important thing is that some kind of decision was required.

Each time an action is repeated, less thinking is called for. Eventually the individual repeats it without conscious thought. The action is semiautomatic. It has become a habit.

This development process is especially true of muscular or "doing" habits. What happens in such cases is that the brain, which makes the decision, sends a "message" through the nervous system of the body. The nervous system transmits the order to the particular muscles involved, and the muscles act as directed. The first time the message is sent, it travels over an unfamiliar path. The muscle is not experienced in the new and unusual act. The process may be slow and awkward.

The connection is made more easily the second time. And with additional practice the muscle reacts to the brain's order so rapidly that conscious thinking is no longer required.

An illustration of this occurs when a person learns to drive a car. At first, intense mental effort and concentration is required for simple actions such as shifting gears or locating the brake pedal. After hours of driving, these same maneuvers become semiautomatic. They are accomplished more skillfully and smoothly and with greater ease.

Habits eliminate the psychological wear and tear of thinking about the same decisions over and over. They permit us to devote our mental efforts to the host of new problems that constantly arise.

Habits can be good or bad. A worker is developing new habits every day he is on the job. The habits may be good or bad; but they are being acquired just the same. The development process described previously applies to both good and bad habits.

Habits are also changeable. Good habits may be replaced by bad ones, and vice versa. A clear understanding of how habits are formed enables you to encourage good habits and discourage bad ones in your workers. It helps you replace poor habits with favorable ones.

How to Encourage Good Habits

1. *Establish the Reason or Necessity for the Desired Action*

In discussing how habits are formed, we mentioned that at the beginning actions are the results of conscious decisions. To encourage a good working habit you must first get the individual to decide in favor of the desired action. The best way is to demonstrate why it is essential, necessary, or helpful. Take time to explain the whys and wherefores in detail. But the important thing is to make certain that the employee understands and agrees to try it out. Once he's reached a favorable decision half the battle is won. As the action is repeated and develops into a habit, it becomes more and more automatic and less and less explanation is required.

2. *Make Sure the Action Is Fair and Reasonable and Applies to Everyone Alike*

If a rule, policy, or direction is to be accepted by those under you and developed into a working habit, it must be fair and reasonable. It should be realistic. It must be capable of being enforced. It should be within the physical or mental capacity of workers. A rule that can't be enforced is worse than no rule at all. For example, a regulation prohibiting employees from going to the washroom during working hours is clearly not realistic — hence it is not enforceable.

By the same token, a rule must apply equally to all if it is to be realistic and enforceable. Not only should it apply to everyone in your department, but it must be in line with over-all policy in force in other departments. It would be difficult, if not impossible, to enforce a "No-Smoking" rule among certain workers in your group if you are letting others get away with it, or if they know that the rule is not being followed in other departments without special reason.

This brings up a problem that often puzzles supervisors: Should discipline be "tight" or lax? Obviously, from what has just been said, it follows that there is no hard-and-fast rule. Standards vary in different companies. It is unrealistic to attempt to set up a "tight" disciplinary policy in your department if the rest of the company operates under a lax system. Similarly it is not wise to follow lax standards in the face of a stern policy. The degree of toughness or laxity is less important than the consistency of the discipline.

3. *Show That the Desired Action Will Satisfy Some Sort of Basic Need Such as Food, Shelter, Comfort, Approval, or Pride*

In addition to giving reasons why the action is necessary from the company's point of view, you must also show them how they, as individuals, will gain by it. You might explain, for instance, how it will make their jobs easier or safer, or improve the quality of their work. Even when it's difficult to show immediate benefit in terms of money, safety, or comfort, it's usually possible to appeal directly to the employee's pride in workmanship — a powerful motivating force. In other words, it is understandable that your men might balk at developing a habit if you simply show why it is important to the company. But they can have little argument if you convince them that it is also beneficial to them.

4. *Once the Action Is Established, Do Not Deviate or Make Exceptions*

Once a favorable action is established, don't deviate from it as it is likely to destroy the habit. Remember that habits are changeable; bad habits can replace good ones if you're not careful. There are times when common sense requires that you make an exception in a particular case. But exceptions should be as few and far between as possible. Otherwise there's the danger that two patterns will be set up in the employee's mind — the right way and the wrong way. This can easily lead to confusion and the employee may forget which is right and which is wrong.

How to Break Bad Habits

There are three rules you can use to discourage bad working habits among your employees:

1. *Interrupt Wrong Actions Immediately and Consistently*

Toleration implies approval. "Looking the other way" when a worker commits a violation encourages bad habits. This is true even if the employee is a first offender. Giving in or making an exception invites a repetition of the violation. Since workers are human, they have a tendency to go as far as they are permitted. Experience shows that the frequency and severity of violations always increase when the supervisor takes a "soft" or tolerant attitude.

Since the employee assumes that silence means assent, he'll continue to act the wrong way. By permitting him to "get away with it" for any length of time, the supervisor is encouraging the formation of a bad habit. At this point, even if the boss intervenes, the worker will probably continue to work the wrong way through force of habit and because he has learned that only once in a while will anything be done to stop him.

On the other hand, correcting an employee when he commits an offense the first time or the first few times will help initiate a good habit. The result is a saving of time, effort, and trouble later on.

2. *Associate the Wrong Action with Something Unpleasant*

Many supervisors complain they don't have the time to give workers the close supervision needed to stop an undesirable habit before it develops. This argument is not valid. It ignores the fact that it is not the time spent correcting a worker that's important, but the sequence of corrections. If an employee knows he can't get away with an undesirable action because the boss will interrupt him or reprimand him each time, he soon decides that the offense isn't worth the trouble. This is true not only of discipline on the job but in other areas as well.

Consider, for example, what happened in a small suburban town that was faced with a serious parking problem. Car owners knew it was against the law to park on the street overnight, but they ignored the rule. The police chief kept getting complaints from local home owners. They demanded that he enforce the law. The chief assigned twelve men to ticket all violators one night a month. When residents pointed out that this system was ineffective because parkers considered it cheaper and more pleasant to pay a two-dollar parking ticket than the seven-dollar monthly rent charged by parking lots, the chief replied that he just couldn't spare the men necessary to enforce the rule every night.

The problem became so critical that the police department decided on an experiment. The chief assigned his parking-ticket detail to tag every car for three nights running. As was expected, tickets given out the first night had no effect; the next evening violators again packed the streets. The third night offenders began to realize that the police meant business and only a fraction of diehards continued to violate the law. By the fourth night the streets were entirely cleared of parkers. Apparently they had decided that sixty dollars a month — the cost of thirty parking tickets — was an expensive and unpleasant way of saving seven dollars a month in parking-lot rent.

The streets continued to remain clear for some time. At the end of three months, however, the chief noticed that overnight parking was again on the increase and he assigned his police detail to ticket parkers for another three nights. Once more this consistent action proved effective. The chief decided to continue the pattern. After a year he totaled up the number of man-days spent enforcing the no-parking ordinance. Much to his surprise, he discovered that the department was spending no more time on the parking detail now than it had under the one-night-a-month plan. The difference was that now it was getting results.

Supervisors are in a position not unlike that of the police chief. How often do we hear a supervisor say wearily: "What am I going to do with this typist? I've told her a dozen times not to use the office telephone for personal calls. I just don't have the time to keep after her every minute of the day." A close examination of this type of disciplinary problem will invariably show that it is the supervisor who is at fault.

Perhaps the supervisor notices for the first time that the typist is making a personal call; but he says nothing. The next day the same thing happens and he feels a little annoyed. When she makes a personal call the third day in a row, he begins to see red and makes up his mind to bawl out the typist if it happens again. And it does.

The typist is shocked to find herself the victim of the boss's fuming. She says to herself: "I've been doing it right along, so why should he make a fuss about it now?" She assumes he is angry because of some personal problem and is only "taking it out on her." To pacify him she promises not to make personal phone calls again. But the next day she is back on the telephone. The supervisor, somewhat ashamed for losing his temper, again overlooks the violation. The pattern is repeated, and the following week another stormy session takes place.

Almost every supervisor who has a family knows that a youngster will never develop habits of tidiness if he is made to pick up his clothes only occasionally instead of consistently. Yet it is surprising how many supervisors who are successful in instilling good habits in their children forget that the same principle applies to training employees.

3. *Replace Bad Habits with Good Ones*

Changing unfavorable habits calls for *positive* supervision. Remember, good habits are essential if proper discipline is to prevail. You cannot leave a vacuum. It is not enough to tell a worker, "You can't do that." You must also tell him what he *can* do, how to do it, and what you expect of him. Make sure that he is able to meet the standards you set.

While it is desirable to give employees certain freedoms wherever possible, make them realize that there is a certain line beyond which they can't abuse those freedoms. Have it understood that if they go beyond this point you are entitled to be firm, strict, or even harsh.

A policy like that is to the employee's advantage. He will feel more secure when he knows exactly what he can and can't do, and he doesn't have to wonder whether he can get away with violating a rule or not. However, just as it is important to interrupt or disapprove a wrong action, remember to commend the worker when he develops a favorable habit.

You set the pace. As a leader you have to set a good example for your worker. An employee may commit a violation that will escape your notice. Yet the same infraction, committed by you, the supervisor, will be seen by twenty pairs of eyes and will serve as a bad example to your men.

LATENESS

Employees who come to work late are a problem. Tardiness is more serious in companies where the job of each employee is interrelated: work can't begin until everyone is present. A major part of the task of controlling tardiness falls on the supervisor since his relations with the worker are closer and more personal.

Lateness is usually handled in one of two ways. Many organizations lay down a hard-and-fast rule for dealing with tardy employees and make no exceptions. If a worker punches in a minute late, he is docked a quarter hour of pay. A second offense may call for stiffer punishment and a third offense may mean suspension. This type of strict policy has its drawbacks. For one thing, it doesn't take into account situations where lateness is unavoidable. Secondly, an overly-strict policy invites absenteeism. The worker who knows he will be tardy may decide that he'd rather take the day off than come in late.

The other extreme is for the company to allow supervisors complete discretion in dealing with tardiness. If the supervisor is easygoing, he may ignore the problem, regardless of what time his employees come to work. In such cases the tendency is for tardiness to increase to the point where even the most punctual employee begins to feel like a fool for getting in on time.

This is the reverse of good discipline. By not taking some sort of action, both the company and the supervisor are training their employees to come late. Moreover, such a negative approach is unfair to the tardy employee because he receives no warning or guidance. Toleration of infractions may actually encourage an individual to be tardy so often that he has to be fired, demoted, or otherwise dealt with severely.

Probably the most effective solution of the lateness problem lies in a moderate approach somewhere between the above extremes. Actually, some company-wide policy is needed so that supervisors will know whether their policies are consistent with the over-all company attitude toward latecomers. Tardiness should be brought to the workers' attention. The supervisor should make it his business to find out why the employee came late. He should examine the worker's past record of lateness. From this and from the excuses given by the worker he can use his judgment in deciding whether the infraction was avoidable. Generally, how often an employee is late is more important than how late he is. There might be a good reason for an employee with an otherwise excellent record to come in an hour late once or twice. But a pattern of continued lateness — even if the tardiness is only a matter of five minutes — may call for more serious measures.

One well-known food company has adopted an effective method of dealing with tardiness. Supervisors are instructed to come in fifteen minutes early each morning and to greet each employee at the department entrance in a friendly, cheerful manner. If an employee is late, the supervisor asks the reason and notes it down in a record book. Although action is taken only in extreme cases, the company's tardiness record is one of the best in the country. The workers, while secure in the knowledge they will be dealt with fairly if a delay is unavoidable, have come to the conclusion that the inconvenience of explaining lateness just doesn't make tardiness worth while.

Tardiness can also extend to recesses like coffee breaks and rest periods. In companies where employees are on a piecework basis, the problem may not be serious. But where the worker is on an hourly basis, there is a tendency to abuse the privilege. Unless the supervisor insists on firm discipline, a ten-minute break may grow to fifteen or twenty minutes and eventually to a half hour. Coffee periods are a privilege, and this fact should be stressed to employees who return late. They should be warned that continued abuse may force the company to cut recess periods out altogether.

ABSENTEEISM

Much of what has been said about tardiness also applies to absenteeism. While it is important to adopt an understanding attitude toward unavoidable absenteeism, you cannot afford to ignore the worker who stays out for personal convenience or just because he "felt like it." You should demand an explanation if for no other reason than to let him know that he's not getting away scot free. If the absenteeism is habitual, you might refer the employee to the industrial relations or personnel department. The employee who finds that he can't simply shrug off his absences but must explain them in detail and submit to questioning by his supervisor and perhaps to one or more higher executives will soon conclude that staying away from work without good reason presents too many complications.

One large oil refinery in New Jersey employing 2,000 workers found that 200 man-days a month were being lost through absenteeism from causes other than sickness and accidents. This represented an increased labor expense because other employees had to cover the work at time-and-one-half pay. Confusion, inferior quality and quantity of work, and other inefficiencies resulted. The refinery personnel manager realized that too little attention had been given to the problem in the past.

He advised employees that all absentees would have to clear through his office before returning to work. Regular violators were interviewed to determine the causes of absences. Several months of this procedure brought the man-days lost each month from 200 down to less than fifty.

ACCIDENT CONTROL

ACCIDENT CONTROL ON THE JOB is given high priority by most organizations. Many supervisors and foremen owe their promotions to their constructive safety efforts. Others have been demoted and even discharged because of continual neglect of safety factors.

Accident prevention is important because *people* are involved. The total physical and mental suffering caused by occupational accidents is staggering. Each year more than fifteen thousand American workers are killed and two million more are maimed or injured in accidents caused on the job. The unnecessary pain and hardship caused by these mishaps are not only suffered by the person who is actually involved. Included in the list of victims are his wife, children, and parents.

There is an *economic* as well as a humane reason for accident control. When a worker is injured on the job, his earning capacity is usually stopped for a time. Even if he or his family collect compensation or insurance, this income seldom makes up for loss of wages. The total loss in this country due to occupational accidents averages $18 billion a year.

When the accident rate goes up, the company loses, too. The premium it has to pay for compensation insurance increases. There is an indirect loss because the company's normal operations have been interrupted. For every dollar spent by companies to pay the direct costs of accidents on the job (hospitalization and compensation), there is an indirect loss of four dollars. This property and production loss by American business and industry is more than 14 billion dollars a year.

Not only the owner or stockholders of the company are affected by loss caused by accidents; it affects the worker group as a whole, and the consumer. Because it has to make up for accident losses, the company is less able to pay high wages to its employees. It is also forced to raise the price of its products or services to the public. When an accident takes place in an office or factory, everyone pays the bill.

A third reason for safety is *employee morale.* It is only natural for a worker to be happier in a company where the accident rate is low. Many firms that have had difficulty attracting new employees or that have suffered from high absentee or "labor turnover" rates traced these problems to low company morale due in part to poor safety records. Accident prevention is so important that sometimes it becomes a basic issue in management-union disputes.

A fourth reason for emphasizing safety is *public relations.* The success of any company depends on the good will of the general public. The public is influenced not only by the quality of a company's products, but by its reputation, policies, and activities. A firm that puts its best foot forward by showing it is concerned with the safety and welfare of its employees is establishing good public relations. A good safety record is a form of advertising that impresses customers, employees, and stockholders. A high accident rate, on the other hand, leads to resentment and ill will among employees and in the community. It may even lead to demands for laws and government intervention. Experience shows that whenever the city, state, or federal government has stepped in to regulate private companies, it is because the companies themselves have failed to carry out their responsibilities properly.

A SAFETY PROGRAM FOR SUPERVISORS

Injuries on the job don't just happen. Every injury is the final link in a chain of events. Before we can have an injury we must have an accident. An accident, in turn, is an unplanned event caused by an unsafe act or an unsafe condition or both.

Let's go back another step. Why do employees act unsafely and often create unsafe conditions? They do so because of some personal defect. For example:

The employee doesn't care. He may not be interested in the job or may not be paying attention. Or perhaps he is purposely ignoring the rules to "get even" with the boss.

The employee doesn't know. Like the amateur carpenter who hits his thumb while trying to hammer a nail into a wall, the employee may simply lack the skill (or knowledge) to do his job safely.

The employee is not able to work safely. A worker may be physically or mentally unable to work safely. He may have some bodily defect such as poor eyesight, hearing, fatigue, or heart trouble. Or angry or otherwise emotionally disturbed.

These personal defects are usually caused by some background condition and may even start outside the job. They include such factors as *inexperience* (the employee may not have been working long enough to gain the experience needed to do the job safely); *home conditions* (worries about money, illness, or other domestic troubles); *personal habits* (lack of sleep, too much drinking, poor eating habits).

Thus, the chain of events leading up to an injury on the job has five links:

Background → *Personal Defects* → *Unsafe Acts or Conditions* → *Accidents* → *Injury.*

Let's take an imaginary case and see how these five links apply:

A maintenance electrician whose child has fallen ill and may require an operation (*background*) reports for work worried and distracted (*personal defect*). He is assigned to crawl under some apparatus to repair a short circuit. He forgets to disconnect and lock out the electrical control switch (*unsafe act*). While he is working under the machine, the regular operator, unaware of his presence, throws the switch sending current through the repairman (*accident*). The man suffers severe burns and shock (*injury*).

The safety problem, therefore, comes down to a question of how to break the chain of events that leads to injuries. The answer is to find the weakest link in that chain and remove it.

With this in mind, let's examine the chain once more. The last two links — accidents and injuries — are *results* rather than causes. Over these we have no direct control.

The first three links — background, personal defects, and unsafe acts or conditions — are *causes*. One of these links should be removed.

What can be done about removing the first link — background? Unfortunately, almost nothing. An employee's home conditions and personal habits are not often subject to outside control.

The same thing is true about the second link — personal defects. They are not subject to outside control; or at best they can be controlled only with great difficulty.

We are left with the third link —unsafe acts or conditions. This is the factor we must try to remove if we are to break the chain leading to accidents and injuries.

The supervisor or foreman is in the best position to eliminate this third link. He is closest to the job and has the opportunity to eliminate it. As the individual who deals directly with the workers, he is the only one close enough to see unsafe acts and conditions taking place from day to day. As a representative of management, he has the authority to control them.

Supervisors often raise the question, "Can we eliminate all unsafe acts and conditions?" The answer is "No." In actual practice it is impossible to do away with them entirely.

Most of us realize, for example, that every time we cross the street we are taking what is known as a "calculated risk." Even when the traffic light shows red in our favor, there is always a possibility that a motorist will ignore the signal and run us down. Yet, because we have to get to the other side of the street, we are forced to take this chance. In effect we are gamblers. We gamble on the law of averages, although by crossing with the light in our favor we improve the odds.

The same thing is true of unsafe acts and conditions in the office or factory. There is always a calculated risk that the employee must take if he is to get certain types of work done.

It is physically impossible for the supervisor or foreman to keep his eye on every worker and on every piece of equipment every minute of the day. So he must accept the fact at the start that there are some unsafe acts and conditions present that he can do little about or that he isn't even aware of.

We know that fortunately every unsafe act or condition does not complete the chain of events leading to an injury-producing accident. We are protected by the law of averages. Insurance companies and mathematicians have found that, according to the law of averages, out of every 330 accidents only thirty result in injuries. Out of the thirty injury-producing accidents, twenty-nine require first aid and only one is serious enough to require hospitalization. By using this knowledge of the law of averages as applied to accidents, it is possible to tell in advance approximately how many accidents will occur in a period of time in a given situation.

What does this mean to the worker on the job? It means that when an unsafe act or condition occurs, Lady Luck is in the corner. She is favoring him with 10-to-1 odds against having any sort of injury-producing accident, and with 330-to-1 odds against his having an accident that requires hospital treatment.

As exposure to the unsafe act or condition continues, Lady Luck slowly begins to desert him, and the odds in his favor become smaller and smaller. Eventually she turns against him and the unsafe act or condition results in an injury-producing accident.

Suppose someone comes up to you with a bottle containing 330 pills that look exactly alike. He tells you that 300 of the pills are harmless salt tablets; twenty-nine pills contain a drug that will make you sick to your stomach; and one pill contains cyanide that will make you seriously ill or kill you. He offers you $25.00 to choose one pill from the bottle and swallow it. What would you do?

If you are a gambler you might decide to accept the offer. You reason that while you might come up with any one of the thirty injurious pills the first time, the odds are 10 to 1 against it. And the odds are 330 to 1 against your choosing the really dangerous cyanide tablet the first time.

But suppose you are offered $25.00 to swallow a pill, provided that if you choose a harmless tablet the first time, you will take another and then another at $25.00 a pill until you are down to the last pill in the bottle? You would most certainly turn down this offer. You know that even if you continue to draw harmless salt tablets, the chance that you will choose an injurious pill becomes greater as the bottle becomes emptier. You are sure to get the bad one if you finish the bottle.

The example of the bottle of pills is similar to the problem of accidents on the job. Compare it with the case of a worker who fails to wear safety goggles while operating a grinder. Although he has not yet been injured, he has often had particles of metal fly off the grinder and miss him by inches. One day a piece flys off and lodges in his eye. He is rushed to the hospital and the eye is removed. Later he is asked about the accident. "I just can't understand it," he says. "I've been working at that grinder without goggles for months and nothing serious happened. Then suddenly I lose my eye, without warning." What this worker didn't realize is that he was given warning each time a particle flew off the grinding wheel and missed him. These particles were like the harmless salt tablets. The accident that caused removal of his eye was the equivalent of reaching into the bottle and finally picking the cyanide pill.

The foreman's or supervisor's job is to see that the employee cuts down on calculated risk as much as possible. He must make certain that unsafe acts and conditions are eliminated wherever possible.

Experience with hundreds of supervisors and thousands of employees proves that a competent supervisor can eliminate in a reasonable and practical way at least *50 per cent of all unsafe acts and conditions*. He is thus able to prevent one-half of all injuries on the job.

Unsafe acts refer to the actions of people. They fall into the category of "human failure." Unsafe conditions, on the other hand, refer to the condition of tools, machinery, clothing, or other inanimate objects. They are "mechanical failures."

Failure to act safely will often lead to an unsafe condition. A worker, for example, may forget to replace the cap on a drum of gasoline. This is an unsafe act. If the drum is allowed to remain uncovered, it sets up an unsafe condition. If fire breaks out as a result of this situation, it is a product of human and mechanical failure. It is caused by both an unsafe act and an unsafe condition.

The great majority of accidents and injuries are caused by unsafe acts rather than by unsafe conditions. In accidents on the job, roughly four are caused by unsafe acts for every one caused by unsafe conditions. The total breaks down like this:

Cause of Accident

Mechanical failure (unsafe conditions) 20 per cent
Human failure (unsafe acts)   78 per cent
Acts of nature (floods, storms, etc.)   2 per cent

UNSAFE ACTS (HUMAN FAILURE)

How can you recognize an unsafe act when it occurs? The following check list describes the possible categories of human failure that can result in an accident. It is based on a careful study made by the American Standards Association and has been used in many successful accident control programs.

1. *Operating without authority. Failure to secure; failure to warn. Operating without authority* includes any unauthorized action such as jumping on a moving vehicle; operating someone else's equipment without permission; using tools or machinery for which the worker has not been trained. *Failure to secure* refers to failure to tie down materials on a loaded vehicle; failure to lock or shut down switches, valves, doors; failure to brake vehicles or other moving objects; failure to shut off equipment when not in use. *Failure to warn* includes failure of the employee to signal properly; failure to place warning signs or tags; or failure to take any action necessary to let others know that he is doing something that may put them in danger.

2. *Operating at unsafe speed.* This includes actions such as running instead of walking; driving an automobile, truck, bus, or other vehicle at above or below safe speeds; feeding or supplying production machines or assembly lines too rapidly; throwing material instead of carrying or passing it; using shortcuts that are unsafe.

3. *Bypassing safety devices.* Disconnecting, removing, plugging, or blocking safety devices; failure to inspect signals, fuses, valves, and other safety devices and keep them in good repair; ignoring signals, warning signs, tags, or other safety instructions.

4. *Using unsafe equipment.* Using tools, machinery, or material that has become defective through wear or tear or abuse, or otherwise made unsafe. This category also refers to the use of hands, feet, or other parts of the body that are used in place of tools or machinery. It includes the use of safe equipment in an unsafe manner, such as gripping tools or other objects improperly or insecurely or using the wrong equipment for a particular job.

5. *Unsafe loading, placing, or combining. Unsafe loading* on a vehicle, platform, conveyer belt, or other apparatus means loading over the safe load limit, loading too high, or loading in such a way as to create a top-heavy or unbalanced load. *Unsafe placing* means placing of tools, equipment, or other materials in such a position as to be in danger of rolling or falling, or where they become an obstruction in work areas, aisles, or other normal-travel routes. It also refers to the placing of hands in, on, or between equipment, or at dangerous points of operation. *Unsafe combining* means mixing chemicals or materials so as to present a hazard. It includes

smoking where flammables are stored; improperly combining acid and water; injecting cold water into a hot boiler; using moving equipment in congested workplaces; or leaving oil, water, or grease on working surfaces that are required to be smooth and dry.

6. *Taking unsafe position or posture.* Lifting or carrying loads improperly; lifting with the body in a twisted or awkward position; walking or working on unguarded beams, girders, and scaffolds; riding on tailboards, on running boards of trucks, or riding in other precarious positions; passing on grades and curves; entering enclosures that are unsafe because of temperature, gases, or exposed power lines; failure to use proper methods of ascending or descending when working in high places; standing in the line of travel of falling or moving objects; taking a position that obstructs the free movement of others.

7. *Working on dangerous or moving equipment when not necessary.* Oiling, cleaning, or adjusting equipment while it is in motion; working on electrically-charged equipment without cutting power; getting on or off vehicles while they are in motion; welding or repairing equipment containing flammable or explosive substances without first cleaning and venting; unnecessary handling of materials while they are being processed on moving machines or conveyer belts.

8. *Horseplay.* Teasing, abusing, or startling fellow-employees; playing practical jokes; boxing, wrestling, throwing material, quarreling, shouting, or making unnecessary noise.

9. *Failure to wear protective devices.* Failure to make proper use of personal protective items like goggles, gloves, safety shoes, hard hats, respirators,

leggings, masks, and aprons; or failure to report defects in such safety apparel. Also, wearing jewelry or unsafe clothing — long sleeves, sweaters, loose clothing or, in the case of women, loose hair styles and high heels.

When An Unsafe Act Occurs

What should you do when you find a worker commiting one of the nine types of unsafe actions listed above? Here are steps you should take in every instance:

1. *Stop* the act immediately and consistently.

2. *Study* the job. If the employee is committing an unsafe act because he thinks there is no other way of doing the job, investigate his work methods.

3. *Instruct.* Once you have decided how the operation can be done with more safety, instruct the worker in the correct method. Tell him how to do it, demonstrate it for him, and let him try it.

4. *Train* the worker in the safe procedure. Check up on him from time to time to make certain he understands it. If necessary, repeat the instructions until you are certain he is trained and will not go back to the old and unsafe method (see chapter on *Training*).

5. *Discipline* the worker only as a last resort and after he has repeatedly shown that he willfully refuses to follow safety rules (see chapter on *Discipline*).

Some supervisors contend that the attitude of the average worker toward safety makes a safety program impossible. They point out that most employees resent safety rules because they think these

way; machines or other equipment where moving parts or other danger points are guarded.

2. *Inadequate guards.* Often a hazard that is partially guarded is more dangerous than if there are no guards. The worker, seeing some sort of guard, may feel secure and fail to take the precautions he would ordinarily take if there were no guards at all.

3. *Defective.* Equipment or materials that are worn, torn, cracked, broken, rusty, bent, sharp, or splintered; buildings, machines, or tools that have been condemned or are in disrepair.

4. *Unsafe design or construction.* This includes machinery, equipment, plant buildings, or facilities that are structurally unsafe because of some error in original planning or construction.

5. *Hazardous arrangement.* Commonly known as "poor housekeeping," this type of unsafe condition includes cluttered floors and work areas; improper layout of machines and other production facilities; blocked aisle spaces or fire exits; unsafely stored or piled tools and material; overloaded platforms and vehicles; inadequate drainage and disposal facilities for waste products.

6. *Improper illumination.* Insufficient light; too much light; lights of the wrong color; glare; or arrangement of lighting systems so that there are shadows or too much contrast.

7. *Unsafe ventilation.* Concentration of vapors, dusts, gases or fumes; unsuitable capacity, location, or arrangement of the ventilation system; insufficient air changes or an impure air source used for air changes; abnormal temperatures and humidity.

8. *Unsafe clothing.* This includes worn-out shoes, torn clothing, oil-stained clothing; safety gog-

gles, face shields, asbestos gloves, aprons, safety shoes, leggings, respirators, safety belts, and other personal safety items that are not available, or are defective or ill-fitting.

What To Do About Unsafe Conditions

1. *Remove* the hazard. If you see a heavy wrench on the edge of a platform where it is liable to fall and injure someone, remove the wrench and put it in its proper place. Or, if you know who left it there, get this person to remove it.

2. *Guard.* Very often a point of danger like high-tension wires or exposed gears on a machine cannot be removed. See to it that the hazard is shielded by screens, enclosures, or other guarding devices.

3. *Warn.* If guarding is impossible, warn of the unsafe condition. Let us say a truck is required to back up across a sidewalk to a loading platform. You cannot remove the sidewalk or build a fence around the truck. You must therefore warn that the unsafe condition exists. You can do this by stationing a man there or by putting up a danger sign. Devices that can be used to warn of unsafe conditions include horns, bells, whistles, signal lights, striped paint, red flags, or signs with the word "danger."

4. *Recommend.* When you cannot remove or guard an unsafe condition on your own, notify the proper authorities about it. Actions like changing the location of machinery, installing sprinkler or ventilating systems, or repairing unsafe areas of the plant itself cannot be taken by the supervisor alone. Among the persons you may have to inform are your own superior, other supervisors, the safety en-

gineer, the maintenance department, or the police or fire department. When such cases arise, you should not merely notify them. Make specific recommendations as to how the unsafe conditions can be eliminated.

5. *Follow up* your recommendations. After a reasonable length of time, check to see if the unsafe condition has been corrected. If it still remains, it is your responsibility to notify the person or persons to whom you made the recommendations.

What To Do When An Accident Occurs

Know whom to call for help when an accident or injury takes place. Know the location of emergency equipment, how to get in touch with the fire department, police, and with the emergency squads of the local gas and electric companies or other utilities. If there is no plant physician, always keep the address and telephone number of a nearby doctor handy. See to it that all injuries, even minor cuts or bruises, receive immediate first-aid attention.

Submit a complete written report of the accident. Many supervisors look on such reports as boring paper work. A common attitude is "After all, the accident is over and done with. Why must I waste time writing it up?" Only through such reports can the company find out whether its accident rate is high or low. When complete reports are kept on file, it is even possible to predict the number and type of accidents that will take place. This is important, because when a company knows what's going to happen, it can do something about preventing it. If a company finds, for example, that there have been an unusually high number of accidents and injuries from gas explosions in recent months, it can start a safety program to eliminate unsafe acts and conditions that may lead to similar occurrences in the future.

What must an accident report reveal? Many companies have their own printed accident forms which merely require filling in the blanks. Where prepared forms are not used, the supervisor must organize his own report and submit it to his superior. This report should answer the following questions:

1. Who was involved, where and when did it occur, why and how did it happen?
2. What machine, tool, or object was involved?
3, What was the unsafe act, if any?
4. What was the unsafe condition, if any?
5. Why was the unsafe act committed?
6. Why did the unsafe condition exist?
7. What have you, as supervisor, done to avoid a recurrence of the accident?
8. What recommendations do you have?

LIFTING AND CARRYING

You will recall that unsafe lifting and carrying was mentioned earlier in this chapter in the list of unsafe acts. It was included in the "taking unsafe position or posture" category. However, injuries due to lifting or carrying accidents are so common that special attention should be given to this problem.

Strains, sprains, and hernia, which usually result from unsafe lifting or carrying, are the most common types of occupational injuries. The United

States Department of Labor finds that they account for about 25 per cent of all on-the-job disabilities in this country.

Such injuries are very painful. They usually occur in the lower back and abdominal region. They often leave permanent effects. And since the average victim is disabled for close to a month, they are also serious from the standpoint of interrupting production.

The usual way for an inexperienced worker to lift a load is to bend his back in a horizontal position and use his lower back muscles for lifting. This is the natural way. But in the case of lifting, it is dangerous and inefficient to do what comes naturally.

The right way is to keep the back straight and as vertical to the ground as possible with knees bent. This is the *unnatural* way. It must be taught. Like using the crawl stroke in swimming or the "touch system" on a typewriter, the right way to lift will seem awkward until skill is developed.

Why should the back be kept vertical when lifting? It gives better leverage. Almost everyone has seen a crowbar used to pry a rock loose. When we lift a weight, we are using the body as a lever instead of a crowbar.

There are three types of levers. They are known as *Class 1*, *Class 2*, and *Class 3* levers. A *Class 1* lever involves the same principle as a child's seesaw. The *Class 2* lever uses the principle of the wheelbarrow. A *Class 3* lever can be compared to a man using a long-handled shovel.

The *Class 1*, or seesaw type of lever, is the most efficient for lifting weights. Archimedes, the great Greek mathematician, was reported to have said that given a long enough lever of this type, a pivot point, and a place to stand, he could lift the world.

When the back is kept vertical, the body becomes a *Class 1* lever. The feet serve as the fulcrum or pivot point. It will then take about fifty pounds of effort to lift a weight of fifty pounds. When the back is bent, however, the fulcrum or pivot point is at hips. It becomes a *Class 3* lever and is less efficient for lifting. And the same fifty-pound weight will take about 200 pounds of effort to lift.

In addition, when the back is vertical, the muscles in the legs are used to put forth most of the effort. These leg muscles are among the strongest in the body and least susceptible to injury. When the back is bent, the lower back and abdominal muscles are made to take the strain. These are the weakest muscles in the body and are most subject to injury.

Here are rules for lifting and carrying:

1. Stand close to the load. Straddle it if possible. The feet should be about twelve inches apart with one foot slightly advanced. This will give you a better balance.

2. The knees should be bent and the back kept straight and vertical, forming as close to a 90 degree angle with the ground as possible.

3. The load should be grasped firmly so it won't slide out of the hands. Before starting to lift, heft or jiggle the load to get an idea of its weight.

4. Start lifting slowly. "Snapping," "breaking," or "jerking" the load should be avoided because this is exactly when a hernia or rupture may occur. Young workers and older workers are especially subject to hernias.

Supervisors often ask, "How many pounds can a worker lift?" There is no definite answer. Some employees can lift more than others. The size and bulk of the load also play a part. The best test is to make certain the worker can start the lift slowly. *If the load won't start slowly, it is too heavy for him.* The supervisor should then get someone else to help or make arrangements to have the load lifted by mechanical means.

5.　When a load has to be carried for a considerable distance, a shoulder-carry is usually effective. The load should not be swung up from the ground to the shoulder. A midpoint — a desk, table, or work bench — should be chosen to rest the load so the lifter can get a better grip. Then the lifting procedure should be repeated to raise the load to the shoulder.

6.　To lower the load, use the lifting procedure in reverse. If a load has been carried on the shoulders, bend the legs, keep the body vertical, and lower the load slowly to a midpoint. When a better grip is obtained, lower it slowly to the ground.

Miscellaneous hints: When long pipes, planks, or ladders are to be carried, the worker should be taught to carry them at a slant, with the front end above the eye level and the rear almost trailing the ground. This will prevent injuries to others who are liable to walk into the load because of blind corners, inattention, etc.

When two workers are required to carry such an object, they should "break" step to avoid bouncing the load. They should also use the same shoulders instead of cross-shouldering. Then, if one trips or drops his end, the other can get clear.

Two or more workers lifting or carrying together should have and use prearranged signals, especially when loading or unloading.

Employees should be continually warned of the danger of muscular injury from twisting, overreaching or getting into awkward positions when lifting, or when working on ladders, scaffolds, or other cramped places.

HOW TO TRAIN EMPLOYEES
SUCCESSFULLY

MANY READERS OF THIS BOOK first learned their jobs by the sink-or-swim method. If this was true in your case, you may recall that you were thrown into the job and told to go ahead as best you could. You probably were your own teacher and learned largely by trial and error. And no doubt you are proud — as you have every right to be — that you managed to make the grade on your own.

We realize today that this old-fashioned system has serious faults. We now know that employees develop much faster and better and become far more efficient when they receive their early training under the eye of a skilled instructor-supervisor.

The amount invested in training a new employee may range from as little as $100.00 for an unskilled worker to thousands of dollars for a skilled worker. Behind each worker is the cost of recruiting applicants, interviewing, testing, selection, indoctrination, paper work, and in many cases a variety of arrangements for medical exams, insurance and benefit plans, etc. Add to this the early training period when administrators and other key people must spend some time with the new employee and you begin to realize the investment made in the new worker.

Proper training pays for itself many times over in both time and money saved. If an employee is instructed carefully, he will avoid many costly errors. Time and again it has been proved that minutes spent at the start in training will save hours and days later on.

You can be reasonably certain that the worker who has been trained properly is doing the job right. You won't have to spend time and manpower correcting his mistakes. There will be fewer accidents as well as less breakage of equipment and waste of materials. What's more, trained workers require far less supervision. This means that you will have more "free time" to spend developing new ideas and methods.

Chapter 1 pointed out that it is not enough for you to know how to do a job well. It is far more important that you know how to get others to do it well. Since you are right "on top" of the job and deal directly with employees, job instruction is basically your responsibility.

Some supervisors try to "pass the buck" when it comes to training. They are found even in large organizations where the importance of training has been established. For example, many companies sponsor vestibule training to give pre-job instruction to new employees. This is simply intended to "break the ice" for the new worker so that he will be better prepared to receive on-the-job training by the supervisor. Yet many supervisors assume that training days are over once the worker has completed a vestibule course. When the new worker makes a mistake or asks for help, the supervisor is likely to say, "Didn't they teach you that in training school?"

Another way supervisors duck the responsibility of training is to assign the trainee to work with an experienced worker who takes over the entire teaching task. This, too, is a bad practice. While it is advantageous to team up a new employee with an older worker to develop skill and know-how, it is a method that can easily be abused. It should be used only after the supervisor himself has carefully instructed the new worker in the operation.

What are the weaknesses in assigning a new employee to an experienced worker right from the start? For one thing, the good worker is not necessarily a good instructor. Second, if he doesn't receive extra pay for taking on the teaching job, he may look upon it as a nuisance. Why should he take the trouble to give away "trade secrets" to a newcomer — knowledge that may have taken him months or years to acquire? How does he know that the new worker won't become a threat to his job security?

Another ineffective way to break in the green employee is to tell him to "Hang around and watch for a week or so." This is bad, psychologically. The new employee is self-conscious because he is "new," and this order adds to his feeling that he is "in the way" and not earning his salt. Also, by hanging around and watching, he may learn the wrong things as well as the right things. He may select as his "model" a poor or inefficient worker and learn the wrong way to do a job. He may see employees breaking rules or company regulations and accept it as common practice. A worker learns best from the supervisor and he is likely to put forth more effort for him than he would for a fellow-employee who has no real authority.

Teaching can be one of the most fascinating phases of your job as supervisor. It has compensations you can't get from anything else. You have the satisfaction of seeing people make progress. Through the student the teacher feels that he accomplishes important and even great things. This pride of accomplishment is the real pay a teacher gets when a talented student becomes a great musician, athlete, artist, or writer. You can get the same type of satisfaction in seeing your pupils — your employees — learn to do a job and get ahead.

The progressive supervisor knows that training never stops; that it should continue as long as the employee is with the company. He knows that even when a worker has mastered one job or one part of a job, it's up to him to help prepare the employee for another. Ability to handle other operations or more complicated work makes the employee more valuable and a credit to his supervisor.

How Job Training Began

Modern job training dates back to World War I. There was a need to train workers as quickly as possible for stepped-up war production. A practical method of instruction that could be used by supervisors was vital. Such a method was developed by the late Charles R. Allen. Later systems of training in business and industry were based largely on his pioneering efforts.

The principles used by Dr. Allen weren't new. They were the results of years of experience by educators, psychologists, and other experts. What Dr. Allen actually did was to sift out from the vast amount of written material on teaching methods the most important findings and principles. Then he organized them into a series of simple and practical steps that could be learned quickly by a supervisor or foreman who had no formal training in teaching a job.

During World War II the nation faced a similar crisis. Once again a method was required for supervisors to use in training large numbers of new workers. The government organized a "Training Within Industry" program which sponsored an even simpler version of Dr. Allen's method. This system went under the name of "Job Instructor Training," or J.I.T. It was geared specifically for the training of supervisors in training new workers, and was used successfully in hundreds of plants by thousands of supervisors and foremen.

After World War II there was a great shift from a wartime to a peace time industrial effort. The Korean War and Viet Nam War and the intervals between continued the need for a method to instruct new employees and to retrain experienced employees.

This need was answered by the development of the method given in this chapter — the "4-Step Method." Although it is similar to J.I.T. and Dr. Allen's system, the "4-Step Method" is more flexible. It can be used not only with the new employee but for training the older worker when new methods, new equipment, new materials, or any new factor is introduced on the job. It also provides a means for the foreman or supervisor to correct errors that the experienced employee may have fallen into the habit of making.

PREPARING TO INSTRUCT

No one is a "born" teacher, but there are certain individuals who turn out to be better teachers than others. The important thing is that the basic techniques of teaching can be learned by almost everyone. The purpose of giving you the "4-Step Method" is not to tell you how to teach a specific job. The purpose is to give you a simple, understandable system which can be used for any type of on-the-job training — whether in the shop, office, school, or even in the home.

The first step in effective teaching is *planning*. Successful teachers often spend more time preparing to teach than in actually giving instructions. Chart every step of the employee's training. Set goals and also dates or times when these goals should be reached. List on a sheet of paper the things you want the employee to learn or do, and the order in which they should be done. Use this job training sheet as a guide to plan your instruction.

Lay out beforehand all tools, equipment, charts, models, diagrams, and other training aids. Objects not required should be removed so that they will not distract the trainee. See to it that the working area is clean and neat and that all safety regulations are met. This is important because the care or carelessness you show at the very start will be remembered and copied by the trainee long after you have finished instructing him in a particular job.

Before you can teach an operation, you must know the work yourself. This doesn't mean that you have to be able to do it better than anyone else in the organization. It means that you must know and understand the best way of doing the whole job from start to finish. Know how to break it up into various parts, and decide the logical order in which to teach each portion of the work. On your job training sheet list the various steps involved in the job.

The most you can expect a new employee to learn at any one time are fifteen simple steps of a job. If a job is complicated and involves more than fifteen simple steps, break it down into sections and instruct the employee in one section at a time. After he understands and does each section reasonably well, the entire job can be tied together.

Consider a supervisor who is instructing a new clerk in the operation of an automatic mimeograph machine. He might break down the job as follows:

1. Place stencil on mimeograph drum.
2. Adjust paper feed tray to proper paper size.
3. Place paper supply in the tray and lock it.
4. Run test sheets through by hand.
5. Check ink supply inside the drum if test sheets are too light.
6. Add ink to drum, if necessary.
7. Adjust drum to raise or lower the stencil as required.
8. Set counting dial for proper number of copies.
9. Disconnect drum handle for automatic operation.
10. Switch on automatic feed.
11. Adjust automatic feed to desired rate of speed.
12. Set drum at proper "stop" position after completing the run.
13. Remove completed copies.

A glance at the thirteen steps shows that while the operation is not simple, it is not too complicated. Therefore, we can assume that for a trainee with normal intelligence and ability, instruction can be given on the entire job without first breaking it down into separate sections.

THE 4-STEP METHOD OF INSTRUCTION

As its name implies, using the "4-Step Method" to instruct involves four basic steps. They are:
1. *Approaching* the employee (whether new or experienced).
2. *Demonstration* by the supervisor.
3. *Performance* by the learner.
4. *Reviewing* the learner's progress.

1. *Approaching the New Employee*

This is the most critical phase of the teaching job. It establishes the mood and mental attitude of the employee. And the employee's mood and attitude determine how quickly he learns and in some cases whether he learns at all. Three things are important: an understanding and sympathy for people; leadership; and the ability to handle people. Although you will find there is one best over-all plan to follow in teaching a certain job, you will also discover that you will have to vary it to suit the personality of the trainee. Make it a point to know your trainee. Is he a slow learner? Does he seem nervous. Does he ask for help when he needs it? How can you relate his previous work to this job?

Put your learner at ease. Introduce yourself and get his name and nickname by which friends call him. Be friendly but not too familiar. The chances are he is self-conscious, nervous, and overeager to "make good." His attention may be distracted by new surroundings, new machines, new procedures, new rules, new bosses, new faces. It is part of your job to help him get over his tenseness as quickly as possible.

A good way to do this is to tell him you realize it will take him awhile to learn. Point out that it took other employees time, too; that you don't expect perfection at first; that you want him to take plenty of time learning properly, rather than rushing and making a lot of errors. Assure him that the operation will grow easier as he goes along and learns each step; that speed will come with experience; and that you will be more interested in how he's doing at the end of two weeks than how he is doing in two days.

You'll also find it helpful to assure the trainee that he'll get all the instruction he needs in learning the job. Remember that the average newcomer is usually afraid of asking questions for fear of appearing "stupid." Encourage him to feel free to ask questions at any time.

In order to help the trainee relax, get him to talk about himself. Let him tell you about his experience, his background, even his sports and hobbies. Gradually swing the conversation around to the particular job at hand. Find out what the trainee knows about it. To make certain you are both talking about the same operation, show him a finished job if you can. Find out whether he has done it before and how skilled he was at it. But don't simply rely on what he tells you in general terms about his background and past experience. Most new workers have an understandable tendency to exaggerate their experience. This is known as "trade bluffing."

Finding out exactly what the trainee knows about the particular job you are going to teach him is vitally important. It enables you to tie in the job with his past experience and gives you a "jumping-off" point at which to start your actual instruction.

When you don't determine the proper "jumping-off" point, you may confuse the trainee by starting at a level he hasn't yet reached and doesn't quite understand. Or, if he has had some experience, you may bore him with a lot of elementary details he already knows.

To discover the exact point at which to start instruction, ask him specific questions about the job. You may even have to test him by having him give you a practical demonstration to show what he can do.

Once you have established the "jumping-off" point, get the trainee personally interested in the job so that he will want to learn it. You can do this in several ways:

First, show the trainee that the job is important, how it fits in with the over-all operation, and why it is necessary. Do this no matter how unskilled, simple, or seemingly unimportant the job is. If you can't prove the job is important, it has no business being there in the first place. Any job that can't be eliminated is important and worth doing.

Second, show the trainee how he as an individual will benefit by learning the job. Tell him exactly how it will add to his experience and skill and make him a more valuable employee. Explain that this experience and skill will give him job security and open up opportunities for advancement and promotion.

2. *Demonstration by the Supervisor*

So far you haven't given the trainee any specific instruction on the job itself. That comes next. Tell and show him how to do the job, step by step. Here are several important principles to keep in mind:

About 85 per cent of our learning is the result of seeing. Ten per cent of learning is the result of hearing. Five per cent results from tasting and feeling. Even the sense of smell plays a part in learning.

Too many supervisors merely try to describe the job to the trainee. They lose the value of the learner's eyes and make their own task that much harder. Wherever and as often as possible, illustrate the job by actual demonstration as well as by sketches, prints, and photographs. Stress the "key points" of the job. A key point is anything that may make or break the job, cause injury or damage, or make the job easier.

In conducting training programs for supervisors, the author has devised a simple demonstration showing the difficulty of using words alone to teach an operation. He lays an unopened pack of cigarettes and a book of matches on a table. Then he tells a supervisor: "Let's pretend I've never seen cigarettes or matches before. I want you to tell me — *but don't show me* — how to smoke a cigarette."

In almost every case, what takes place is about as follows:

Supervisor: "Pick up the pack of cigarettes."
Author picks up the book of matches.

Supervisor: "I said pick up the cigarettes, not the the matches.

Author: "Oh, I get it. The other object is the pack of cigarettes. You see, I've never seen cigarettes or matches before."

Author lays down the matches and picks up the cigarettes.

Supervisor: "Now open the pack."

Author attempts to open the pack by ripping it in half.

Supervisor: "No, no. You'll break the cigarettes that way. See that little red cellophane tab at the top of the pack? Pull it. Then tear a piece of that silver foil off the upper corner."

Author does this and exposes several cigarettes.

Supervisor: "Now pull out a cigarette."

Author tries to extract one of the tightly packed cigarettes, but has difficulty.

Supervisor: "You'll find it much easier if you tap the bottom of the pack first."

Author taps the pack and several cigarettes creep up. He pulls one out.

Supervisor: "Now put it in your mouth."

Author crams entire cigarette in his mouth like a stick of gum.

Supervisor: "No. You're doing it wrong. Just hold about a quarter-inch of the cigarette between your lips. Let the rest of it dangle out of your mouth. Now reach for the matches . . ."

The above demonstration shows how hard it is to give instruction without showing how or using visual aids. It shows the importance of stressing key points — in this case pulling the red tab and tapping the bottom of the cigarette pack. It proves the need of

explaining the job in terms the trainee can understand. Things are often clear to us because we know
the details, but they are not clear to the other fellow.
Ask yourself: "Did I make things clear? Really
clear? Did I explain the job in terms the trainee
could understand? Did I make the mistake of assuming the trainee knew something he didn't? Did I
expect him to understand things that would have
confused me when I first came on the job?"

Even simple words can be confusing if they are
"trade words." In all jobs there are terms that have
a special meaning for employees. The learner may
not yet understand these trade words. If you use
them, make certain you have explained them so that
the meaning is clear.

One way to avoid these mistakes is to use the job
training sheet you prepared before approaching the
trainee. This sheet is simply a step-by-step breakdown of the operation to help you decide the best
order in which to teach it. You can use it as a guide
to help you note key points and to explain the job in
such a way that it won't be over the trainee's head.
Here is how to do it:

Next to each step listed in the breakdown, write
the things the trainee must know before he can be
expected to perform the step. Mark with a "KP"
(key point) each item that can be classified as: (1)
it makes or breaks the job, (2) may cause injury or
damage, or (3) makes the job easier.

While explaining and demonstrating the various
steps in the operation, refer to your guide. Make
sure the trainee knows what he is required to do in
each step. In this way you'll be explaining the job
in terms the trainee can readily understand.

Let's refer to our cigarette experiment again. If we broke down the operation, the beginning of our guide chart might look like this:

Steps in the Job	Trainee Must Know
1. Pick up cigarette pack	Identification of objects KP
2. Open pack	Red tab should be pulled KP
3. Remove cigarette	Tap bottom of pack KP
4. Place cigarette in mouth	Only one-quarter inch between lips KP
5. Etc. . . .	

Instruction should be given slowly, clearly, and in a distinct voice. Remember, what's slow for you may not be slow for the trainee. Don't try to show off how fast you can do the job. It's a good idea to go so slowly that it will seem exaggerated to you. If the learner appears to be having trouble catching on, don't put him down as a numbskull. Give him a fair chance. He may be suffering from first-day or first-job jitters. Or he may be afraid to ask questions for fear of appearing stupid. Think back to when you were learning. Did you catch on immediately? Weren't you a bit confused?

Whatever happens, don't lose your patience. Once you do, you lose the trainee's respect and you'll really have your troubles teaching him.

As you explain and demonstrate, observe the trainee closely. Watch his facial expressions. These expressions, together with what he says will help you decide whether he understands you. Don't let his attention wander. Break in with a question every so often. The questions should have but one purpose: to hold his attention. Don't ask the trainee to describe the job back to you because at this stage it would merely confuse him.

3. *Performance by the Learner*

The trainee is now ready to "take over the controls." He is prepared to put to work for the first time all the things you taught him. If you have carried out the previous steps carefully, you can expect him to approach his "dry run" with enthusiasm. But don't be concerned if he is nervous. In his eagerness to please he might become all "thumbs" or suffer a slight attack of stage fright.

In the beginning let the trainee do the job without interruption. Don't interfere if he pauses momentarily to collect his wits or to think about his next move. Don't worry if he does the job clumsily at first. People aren't born with skill. It must be developed through practice.

However, the moment you notice the trainee is about to make a mistake, *stop him.* There is a good reason for this. If you allow him to do the job wrong even once, the error may start a habit that is hard to break.

Some supervisors do just the opposite. They like to trap a learner. They purposely remain silent while he commits a blunder and let him complete the operation. Only after the entire job comes out wrong do they bring the error to his attention. They think he'll learn by the bad experience.

Such a practice is poor policy. It usually makes the newcomer nervous and embarrassed. It confuses him and may start a bad habit. Since he has been allowed to do the job the wrong way at least once, there are now two patterns in the back of his mind: the right way and the wrong way. Later he may forget which is which and continue making the same mistakes.

When you stop a learner because you see he's going to make an error, let him try to figure out what he is doing wrong. Let him think about the mistake for a little while. If he still hasn't caught it or can't recall the right way, give him a hint by asking him one or two leading questions. But encourage him to work out the problem himself. Self-correction is always better remembered than direct correction by the instructor. It also adds to the person's confidence and gives him a certain sense of satisfaction.

After the trainee has run through the operation the first time, have him repeat it several times for practice. Again, don't interrupt him except to correct mistakes. When you feel he is reasonably familiar with the job, you are ready to test him.

Tell him to go through the operation once more. But this time ask questions. As he proceeds with each step, have him explain *what* he is doing and *why*. This will reveal his understanding of the job. Up to now he may have been doing the operation simply by imitating your demonstration without really knowing what he was doing. If he can't explain a step, give him additional instruction until he can.

There's an old saying: "The scientific man knows why; the practical man knows how; the expert knows why and how." It's to your advantage to train a person to be an expert at the job, so be certain he knows the *why* as well as the *how*.

As the new employee progresses, encourage him and build up his self-confidence. Be honest about it. Don't say he is doing an expert job or performing the operation as well as you can. You and he both know that it's still far too early in the game for him to have developed real skill. If you tell him he's getting perfect results, he'll sense that you're insincere and merely trying to flatter him. The right way is to give him credit for making progress. Let him know he's coming along nicely. If you can't honestly give him credit for progress, it means he hasn't been learning. And if he hasn't been learning, it's safe to assume that you're at fault. You'll then have to go back to the earlier steps and give him additional instruction. A good motto to keep in mind is: "If the learner hasn't learned, the instructor hasn't taught."

4. Reviewing the Learner's Progress

The new employee should now be able to stand on his own two feet. He should feel he can do the job without having someone hang over his shoulder every step of the way. Before leaving him alone, however, tell him to let you know if he gets into trouble or needs help. If it's impossible for you to be around, designate an experienced worker to whom he can go. Let this employee know what's going on.

Return at frequent intervals to check the trainee's progress. Examine his work for errors before he has a chance to cause much waste or damage. Don't give him the impression you've forgotten about him. Encourage him to ask questions.

Taper off gradually on close supervision. If the learner is doing his job well, leave him alone for a longer period. As he grows more and more reliable, increase the time-span of your "checks" until you feel safe in letting him proceed under normal supervision.

Normal supervision doesn't mean you can now consider him an experienced worker. On your regular inspection trips, pay him particular attention. There may be weaknesses in his performance which aren't apparent during his first few weeks on the job but which show up later. And as the newcomer improves, set a new and definite goal for him to strive for.

A supervisor will often tell an employee, "You're making progress. Good work. Keep it up." Or, "See what you can do this time." This is a poor approach. It's like telling the worker to walk for three miles around and around the block. Since it doesn't give him a mark to aim for, he'll get tired and bored quickly. Instructing him to try to do a definite amount of work in a given time, however, is akin to telling him to walk to a specific objective three miles away to deliver a package. He has a clear goal ahead of him, and that helps to make the job interesting and more purposeful.

Goals must not be too hard or too easy to achieve. They should set a steady and reasonable pace and should be attainable if the trainee applies himself diligently. This is called the principle of "measured progress" and is based on the fact that specific goals are an incentive to learning.

Encourage the new worker to think about his job outside of working hours. Urge him to read books, attend special courses offered by the company or educational institutions. Stimulate him to keep ahead of his job by putting in extra effort on his own. Make him realize that while you will give him all the help you can, only he can determine what his future with the organization will be.

What did you learn? When you teach a new employee, the learning isn't confined to the trainee alone. After teaching each job, ask yourself, "What have I learned? What can I do to improve the training method next time?" Make notes. Outline for your own benefit how you would more perfectly and effectively handle the task in the future.

Long or Short Sessions?

Short training sessions are preferable to long ones. Educators report that a certain amount of learning takes place between the actual sessions themselves because the trainee has a chance to mull over the instruction he has been given. Thinking about the job between sessions promotes better understanding. Anyone who has learned to drive a car recognizes that ten one-hour periods are more effective than five two-hour sessions or two five-hour periods. In addition, breaking up your instruction into short sessions helps prevent fatigue and boredom, two arch-enemies of learning.

Learning Speed

Speed in learning a job varies with the individual. Some persons learn more slowly than others. Some learn faster. When a trainee learns quickly, there is a tendency for the supervisor to think, "He catches on quickly. He'll make an excellent worker." This is not necessarily so. There is no connection between how fast a newcomer learns and his ultimate value as a worker. Some trainees learn fast at the start and then reach a saturation point beyond which they cannot go. Or else they may be temperamental or easily bored — two traits that make for an unsatisfactory employee. The slow learner, on the other hand, may be dependable and conscientious. He may develop speed and skill as he gains experience, and turn out to be an excellent worker.

It's a good policy not to judge a person on his learning speed alone. Consider his general attitude. Is he eager to learn? Does he always give his best efforts? Does he get along well with others? Even if it takes him slightly longer to catch on, does he generally wind up with a thorough understanding of the job?

Never urge the learner to go faster than accuracy permits. Concentrate on developing accuracy rather than speed. Even if he wants to do the job fast, slow him down if he makes mistakes. Keep reminding him and yourself that while speed develops with experience, accuracy must start at the very beginning.

LANGUAGE BARRIERS

You may be called upon to train a worker of foreign background who speaks little or no English. In some places such workers comprise a large part of the labor force. This is true, for example, in the farming areas of Texas and on the West Coast. When a language barrier exists try to find an amateur interpreter to help you teach the job. But with or without an interpreter, lean heavily on actual demonstration and visual aids. Depend on the trainee's eyes to do most of the learning — at least until his knowledge of English improves.

GROUP INSTRUCTION

Try to give job training on an individual basis. A trainee will always learn more easily if you concentrate on him alone. Sometimes, however, when a company opens a new plant, undergoes expansion, or operates on a seasonal arrangement, you may be faced with the task of training an entire group of new employees. Start the entire group on some useful work and then try to stagger your schedule and instruct each newcomer individually.

If this is not possible, arrange to give to a group the first two steps of the "4-Step Method" (*Approaching the New Employee* and *Demonstration by the Supervisor*). The last two steps (*Performance by the Learner* and *Reviewing the Learner's Progress*) will have to be handled on an individual basis.

If you don't have time to follow through the last two steps for each employee in the group, assign several experienced workers to help you. First find out if it is in keeping with union regulations —assuming your workers are unionized. But maintain personal supervision over the entire training program. Brief your "assistants" carefully and check often to make sure they are doing the training job correctly.

APPROACHING THE EXPERIENCED EMPLOYEE

A real problem in training is encountered with the experienced employee. The man who has developed bad practices needs special attention. He may violate safety rules, turn out inferior quality, or let down on his work output. If a worker is not performing the way he should — be he a new or old employee — he needs training.

When the man or woman to be trained is an experienced employee, there are three types of situations you may meet:

1. The employee doesn't know how to do the job because something new has been added such as a new method, new equipment, new materials, or a new location. He may have the know-how but lacks skill, dexterity, or coordination.

2. The employee is unable to do the job the new or correct way because of some handicap such as poor eyesight, heart trouble, or emotional disturbance. A worker who is worried, irritated, or emotionally disturbed, cannot put his mind on his work. For example:

A girl feeding a machine caused a high percentage of rejects because she pushed the material too far into the machine. A checkup revealed a visual defect in her depth perception. The eye doctor prescribed the proper corrective eyeglasses and the trouble ceased.

A maintenance man ran into a series of personality clashes — fighting with all the production people he contacted. Eventually the supervisor got to the heart of the problem. The maintenance man misunderstood the overtime-hours procedure and thought he was getting a raw deal.

3. The employee knows the right way but lacks willingness and interest in doing the job.

When the employee doesn't know the new way (Situation 1), your task is simply a matter of following the "4-Step Method," using an approach similar to that for the new worker. Since your pupil is experienced, you should have little trouble determining the jumping-off point at which to start instruction. Explain how the new method, new machine, or new material will improve his job and benefit him by enabling him to turn out better work with less effort, and perhaps earn more money. (See the chapter on "How to Simplify Work Methods.")

Where the employee has some handicap that prevents him from adapting himself to the new or correct way (Situation 2), find out whether the trouble is temporary and can be corrected. If it cannot be corrected, you may have to reassign the worker to a job where his handicap is not an obstacle to good performance.

Experience shows that the most frequent problem is Situation 3 — the worker knows the right way but is indifferent or apathetic. This calls for the psychological approach.

The approach you use is important. As with the case of new workers, the approach sets the stage for learning. It establishes the employee's mood and mental attitude and determines how quickly he'll accept the instruction or whether he'll accept it at all.

Unlike the case of a new worker, you won't have the task of putting the experienced worker at ease. Chances are he's already at ease, perhaps too much so. One problem may be to put yourself at ease so you won't lose your self-control and blow up.

A seasoned employee might resist your attempts to correct him because he feels you are criticizing him rather than his work. This may happen when personal criticism is furthest from your mind. Yet the employee may not understand this. Even when he knows he is doing the job wrong, he assumes a direct order to change is a form of criticism. He feels he has a right to do as he pleases, having earned this "privilege" by being on the job a long time.

When you correct him, his reaction is likely to be, "I was here before you came and I'll be here after you've gone." He is apt to follow up this defiant attitude with one of several alibis:

"This is the way I've always done it."

"The other supervisor told me to do it this way."

"It's easier and more comfortable doing it this way."

"Others are doing it this way. Why pick on me?" (A feeling of persecution.)

"That's the way you showed me."

The worker is so busy defending himself, he doesn't have the time or inclination to accept logical reasons why he should correct his ways. He has been pushed into a corner. His vanity, pride, and self-confidence have been injured. And his natural reaction is to hit back.

Other employees will swallow their resentment and do as they are ordered. But they do it unwillingly. They are burning to "get even" the first chance they have. Eventually they slip back to the wrong way, slow down on the job, or break company rules or safety regulations.

Whether the worker shows his resentment openly or secretly, you are the loser. You have failed to get the employee to correct himself.

How can you avoid such situations? Don't barge in with direct or abrupt corrections which may put the employee on a spot where he feels called upon to hit back. Use an indirect approach, thus giving him a chance to save face or to correct himself without admitting that he has been doing the job wrong.

You might, for example, use a gentle reminder: "This method looks hard. I wonder if there is an easier way of doing it." Or could you transfer the blame for the mistake to something else, preferably an inanimate object?

Let's assume you are a production supervisor and notice a worker placing labels on the product in a sloppy manner. The labels are not straight with the edges and excess glue is being applied. Instead of ordering him to be more careful, you might ask him if he has enough light to see the proper alignment and if the glue is too thick for proper application. Adjusting the lighting and thinning the glue may actually help, but the important thing is that since you have not accused him, he has no need to defend himself. You've managed to bring the errors to his attention so that he'll strive to be more careful in the future.

You might assume the blame yourself. Volunteer to reinstruct the employee by saying: "Maybe I didn't explain this point." Or, "Perhaps I went too fast when I taught you this job."

You may meet an employee who is doing the job wrong because he is disturbed by some personal problem. If you suspect this is the case, investigate further. Ask him some friendly, personal questions. Volunteer to listen to his troubles. In nine out of ten cases he will repay you for your patience and sympathy by making a real effort to correct his job errors.

HOW TO SIMPLIFY WORK METHODS

Every job can be done in different ways. But a careful study of any job, even a simple one like hammering a nail into a board will show that there is always a "best" way of doing it. "Best" means how well, how quickly, how easily, how cheaply, how safely, and how comfortably the job can be done.

Some persons seem to be born with a knack for finding the "best" way. Take two housewives, both of whom have the same size family and same size house to care for. One woman may take six hours a day to do all her housecleaning, shopping, and cooking. The second woman will do the same amount of work, and do it as well, in only four hours. Why? Not because of special training, but because she seems to have developed an ability for doing housework efficiently.

The same is true of supervisors. Whether in the house, shop, or office, there is a pattern — a group of rules — involved in doing any job efficiently. Some supervisors, like the second housewife, acquire this pattern naturally and with little effort. Other supervisors take time and effort to learn it. The important thing is that *it can be learned,* even if a person is not "born" with it.

Finding the "best" way of doing a job depends upon how "methods-minded" you are. If you don't come by the skill naturally, study and learn and apply to specific jobs the rules for improving methods given in this chapter. You'll find that through constant use you will be applying the pattern by force of habit to every job that has to be done.

Before discussing the actual rules, let us first examine how methods-improvement — also known as "work simplification"— developed and some of the reasons why such a system is valuable.

The "Speed-up"

The factory system, as we know it today, started about a hundred years ago. The main factors in its growth were: 1) the invention of machines that made "mass production" possible; 2) the demand for more products at less cost.

As these factors developed, competition grew between different factories making the same type of goods. Factory owners paid more and more attention to increasing production. Each owner was concerned with the problem of manufacturing more goods at less cost than his rival so that he could sell his product more cheaply.

The simplest and most obvious answer was to "push" the workers to produce more. The owners found they could get away with this. They knew they held the advantage and so did the workers. One method used was to speed up the production line, setting a production pace which the worker had to follow. Another method was to increase the quota of work. The employee was simply told to produce more in the same amount of time for the same wage, or get out!

Workers began to fight back. They organized into unions to protect themselves against the speed-up. Reports of horrible working conditions spread to the public. Enlightened bosses, realizing the evils of the speed-up, outlawed it in their plants and looked around for other ways to increase production.

THE "EFFICIENCY ENGINEERS"

About fifty years ago a group of industrial engineers introduced what soon came to be known as "scientific management." Their idea was simple. In every industry and business, they reasoned, there was a great deal of waste and inefficiency. By improving methods and eliminating unnecessary operations, production would increase and costs would drop.

While touring a coal mine, one man found that the miners used very large shovels. Large shovels, he was told, enabled each miner to scoop up more coal. But he saw that lifting large loads of coal caused the workers to tire easily and forced them to stop for frequent rests.

This efficiency pioneer convinced the mine owner to introduce smaller shovels. There was an immediate increase in production. The pioneer found that while each scoopful of coal was smaller, the miners could work steadily so that the total amount shoveled during a working day was much greater. There were also additional savings in operating costs because of fewer production interruptions caused by cases of rupture, backstrain, and other injuries.

This early type of efficiency engineering led to more careful studies. Factory owners learned that the time and effort they spent developing efficient methods more than paid for itself in production increases and savings in the cost of labor and material.

There was great enthusiasm among companies for this type of scientific management. The efficiency expert who wandered about a plant or office making entries in his little black notebook was a common sight. But employees made bitter jokes about the "efficiency boys" who invaded factories and stuck their noses over the worker's shoulder and into every operation. What employees resented and feared most about the efficiency expert was that each visit might mean wholesale layoffs and outright discharge of workers who were considered unnecessary.

The supervisor and worker of those years found a way to deal with the "efficiency engineer." They quietly sabotaged the new "efficient" methods which the expert introduced. Machines suddenly "broke down" and unexplained bottlenecks developed.

It did not take long for managers to see that they could not ram efficiency down the worker's throat. They began to realize that efficient operation could only be introduced with the full cooperation of the employee and the middle-manager.

The speed-up failed for two reasons: Work quotas were set at the whim of the boss and were not based on scientific knowledge of how much physical labor an employee was able to do. Nor was the human side of men at their jobs taken into account.

Efficiency engineering was based on scientific principles. It included a study of such things as body motion, reaction time, and the worker's physical limitations. Like the speed-up, scientific management overlooked the "human factor." It did not take into account that the employee would naturally oppose any system that might cause him to lose his job. Nor did the efficiency engineer foresee how much the worker would resent new methods that meant greater profits for the boss and nothing extra in his own pocket. The efficiency movement also overlooked a simple rule of human nature: People are suspicious and resentful of outsiders — in this case the efficiency expert — who suddenly enter upon the scene and tell them what to do and what not to do.

Methods Improvement

A new method was introduced just before the outbreak of World War I. This was known as "methods improvement" or "work simplification." Like efficiency engineering it was based on scientific principles. Many of the principles used were borrowed from the earlier work of the efficiency experts. But work simplification also took into account human factors. It introduced improved methods not at the expense of the employee but with his full knowledge and cooperation. Because of the need for increased war production, the new system of methods improvement grew by leaps and bounds during World War I. And it has continued to develop ever since.

The story of the growth of American business and industry is really one of methods improvement. When carried out wisely, methods improvement helps the employer gain more profits. It also enables the consumer to buy more quality goods at a cheaper price, thus raising his standard of living. It provides more opportunity for employment and helps the worker earn higher wages in less time and with less effort. When methods are improved, everyone is served — the employer, consumer, and employee.

In simple terms, methods improvement or work simplification is a practical working procedure to help the supervisor make the best use of men, machines, and materials. It is not intended to make people work harder or faster. On the contrary, it enables them to do more and better work with less effort and in less time. As a direct result of improved methods, the typical American employee today works a total of 2,000 hours a year as contrasted with the worker of 1850 who labored 3,600 hours annually. Simplifying work increases quality and quantity of production by improving job methods and reducing waste of time, energy, equipment, and materials.

How does methods improvement or work simplification differ from the previous systems discussed? We've already mentioned that unlike speed-up and efficiency engineering, methods improvement takes the human factor into account. This is done in several ways:

1. As improved methods are introduced, they are explained thoroughly to the worker. He develops understanding and acceptance instead of resentment. In many cases ideas are developed from the worker's suggestions.

2. If the worker's job is eliminated, he is reassigned instead of laid off. In this respect work simplification is the opposite of "efficiency management." When a temporary "dislocation" occurs, work simplification provides that the employee be

retrained and assigned to another job while the company continues to pay him. The company can afford to do this because it knows from experience that for every job eliminated through improved methods, the increased production that results from lower prices and increased demand creates several new jobs.

3.   As improved methods increase production and cut costs, the employee is given a share in the added profits. This is done through one or more arrangements. The worker may be given incentive pay, profit shares, bonuses for reaching production quotas, or he may be paid on a straight piecework basis. He has a personal interest in seeing better methods and increased production developed.

4.   Improved methods are introduced through the existing company setup. In work simplification, unlike efficiency engineering, new methods are not imposed by "outside" experts who go directly to the worker and tell him what to do. Instead, supervisors and other representatives of management are first trained in work simplification. They, in turn, pass on improved techniques to the worker. The employee is taught the "best" way by persons he knows and works with every day rather than by a stranger whom he is likely to distrust.

5.   Employee suggestion plans often provide a good channel for improvements.

A PLAN OF METHODS IMPROVEMENT FOR SUPERVISORS

When a company sets up a production job, staff engineers usually work out the plans. They are helped by foremen and supervisors in developing methods to be used. The reason for this is that few jobs, even in large companies, are so mechanical that the industrial engineer or technical expert can cope with every detail or foresee every problem that may arise. This is also true in small companies, offices, or stores.

The supervisor, foreman, or office manager is usually in a good position to improve work methods. He is the one to decide how the job is to be done, how the work should be laid out, which tools and equipment should be used, what instructions are to be given to the employee.

Understanding how to simplify work methods requires an open mind. As it was pointed out earlier, it calls for you to become "methods-minded." That means you must continually think in terms of improving present methods. But in order to do this, you must recognize that there is room for improvement in any job; that the "best" way to do a job is not always the usual or accepted way. Nor is it necessarily the obvious way.

Here's a simple example: You are handed an electric toaster and three slices of bread and asked to toast them in the least possible time. The toaster is the old-fashioned manual type that requires you to turn over the two slices as the sides are toasted. Assume that the toaster is ready for use and that a side requires thirty seconds to toast. What method would you use?

The answer usually given is: Toast two slices on both sides (sixty seconds); then toast the third slice on both sides (sixty seconds). The total time is 120 seconds.

Is there a quicker way? A bit of "methods thought" on the problem reveals there is. Since there are three slices of bread, six sides have to be toasted. Insert two slices and toast one side of each (thirty seconds). Then, instead of reversing both slices, reverse only one, remove the other slice, replace it with the third slice and toast again (thirty seconds). You now have one fully toasted slice and two slices with one toasted side each. Toast these remaining two sides (thirty seconds). The total time required is ninety seconds — thirty seconds less than the "accepted" method.

Five-Step Plan

Methods improvement requires orderly thinking as well as an open mind. In simplifying a job, follow these five steps in order:

Step 1.   Pick the job to be improved.
Step 2.   Break down the job on paper.
Step 3.   Question each detail of the job.
Step 4.   Work out a better method.
Step 5.   Put the new method to work.

Step 1.   *Pick the Job to Be Improved*

The fact that there is room for improvement in any job does not mean that you should start out to simplify "just any job." Since your time is valuable, use it to greatest advantage by starting first on those jobs most in need of improvement.

Clearing up these "sore-spots" will mean the greatest benefit in terms of over-all efficiency. In addition, noticeable benefits will encourage further job-improvement effort.

Finding the sore spot may not be as simple as it sounds. Things that need improvement are not always obvious. It is easy to walk by the same bad situation day after day without seeing it. To determine what needs to be improved most requires that you study the over-all picture carefully.

Most sore spots fall into one of these categories: Bottleneck jobs; time-consuming jobs; hazardous spots; jobs that require a lot of "chasing around" for materials and tools; or jobs that involve excessive paper work.

Check the operations you supervise. Ask yourself, "Which activity needs improvement the most?" Once you have decided, write it down and note the reasons for your choice. Review the matter with your boss. Discuss the "hot" spots with him. See if he agrees that you have chosen wisely. In this way he'll know what you're doing and will cooperate later on in making any changes you decide are necessary to clean up the trouble.

Step 2.   *Break the Job Down on Paper*

Once you have picked the job, break it down on paper. In order to analyze a complete process, it must be put down detail by detail. Then you can successfully think about it. Since most of us don't bother to remember details, it is a good idea to make the breakdown by actually observing the job. In this way all unnecessary or wasted steps can be recorded for study later on.

For example, if you asked a secretary to give you a step-by-step picture of her actions in typing a letter, she would probably report that she slipped the paper in the typewriter and typed the letter. Yet if you asked her to list each step *at the time she did it*, the report might read something like this:

Walked across the room to closet
Opened cabinet
Took out unopened package of stationery
Opened package
Withdrew about fifty sheets
Replaced package
Closed cabinet door
Walked back to desk
Threw wrapping paper into wastepaper basket
Opened desk drawer
Withdrew carbon paper and two "onionskin"
    sheets for carbon copy
Closed drawer
Placed carbon between original sheet and onion-
    skin
Tapped sheets on desk to even edges
Placed sheets in typewriter
Started typing letter
Made erasure and corrected error
Finished letter
Read letter for errors

This type of breakdown, giving the step-by-step details in any process, is known as a *Flow Process Chart*. It shows how the job is being done. Many companies use printed forms for this purpose. If such forms aren't at hand, a blank sheet of paper can be used.

How to Prepare A Flow Process Chart. The first step in preparing a Flow Process Chart is to be sure you are really breaking down the right job. Write down exactly what it is.

Choose the subject for your Flow Process Chart and stick with it. Pick a person, part, or paper form, depending upon which goes through the entire process you are working on. Once you choose the subject, don't change. Each detail you put in your list must be on that one subject.

To be sure you cover the ground you want to cover and no more, pick a starting and ending point.

Next, write a brief description of each detail step by step and number it in order. You will get the complete picture only if you list every detail, no matter how brief or temporary.

In Flow Process Charts each detail falls into one of four categories. Each category has a symbol known as a Therblig. Therbligs were devised by the late Frank B. Gilbreth and his wife, Lillian M. Gilbreth. These symbols and the categories they stand for are:

O—Operation (sawing, filing, typing, wrapping, etc.)

o—Transportation (walking, driving, carrying, etc.)

□—Inspection (weighing, checking, measuring, proofreading, etc.)

△—Storage (waiting for delivery, lying in file basket, etc.)

After finishing your list, classify each detail into one of the categories given above and mark it with the proper symbol. Place next to each detail the time in minutes it takes to complete. If the detail falls in the "transportation" category, note the distance of the move in feet.

At the bottom of the chart write the total time, total distance, and total number of each type of symbol.

Suppose you want to prepare a Flow Process Chart covering the delivery of a desk from a storeroom to an office upstairs. If no printed forms are available, your chart would probably look like this:

Activity: Delivery of Desk from Storeroom to Room 413.

Present Method

	Distance (Feet)	Time (Min.)	Symbol	Steps
1.			△	In storeroom
2.		.5	O	Place on hand truck
3.	100	.5	o	To elevator
4.		.5	△	Wait for elevator
5.		.5	O	Roll truck on elevator
6.	60	.5	o	To fourth floor
7.		.5	O	Roll truck off elevator
8.	200	1.1	o	To room 413
9.		.5	□	Inspect for damage
10.		.5	O	Take off hand truck
11.		1.1	O	Push desk into place
Total:	360 ft.	6.2 min.	5 — O	
			3 — o	
			2 — △	
			1 — □	

In place of a Flow Process Chart, a *Flow Diagram* is sometimes used. This is a plan or layout of the area drawn to scale over which you indicate by a line the movement of the item which is being followed on the Flow Process Chart. The Flow Diagram is a help in visualizing the job when travel and

FLOW PROCESS CHART
SEE INSTRUCTIONS ON REVERSE SIDE.

ACTIVITY CHARTED Widget Delivery

CHART NO._____ SHEET_____ OF_____

CHARTED BY Bertram Puddle

SUBJECT CHARTED Widget

DATE_____ 19____

CHANGE CALLED FOR

COMPANY_____

PLANT_____

DEPT._____

SHIFT_____ SECTION_____

SUMMARY

METHOD	PRESENT	PROPOSED	SAVING
NO. OF OPERATIONS			
NO. OF TRANSPORTATIONS			
NO. OF STORAGES			
NO. OF INSPECTIONS			
MAN HOURS OR MINUTES			
DISTANCE TRAVELED			
TOTAL COST			

COST OF CHANGE TO PROPOSED METHOD

DIST. IN FEET	TIME IN MIN.	OPERATION / TRANSP. / STORAGE / INSPECT.	DESCRIPTION OF PRESENT METHOD	DIST. IN FEET	TIME IN MIN.	OPERATION / TRANSP. / STORAGE / INSPECT.	DESCRIPTION OF PROPOSED METHOD
		○ ○ △ ☐	In bin	1		○ ○ △ ☐	
	.5	○ ○ △ ☐	Picked up	2		○ ○ △ ☐	
8		○ ○ △ ☐	To truck	3		○ ○ △ ☐	
	.5	○ ○ △ ☐	Place on truck	4		○ ○ △ ☐	
75		○ ○ △ ☐	To elevator	5		○ ○ △ ☐	
	.5	○ ○ △ ☐	Take off truck	6		○ ○ △ ☐	
	.5	○ ○ △ ☐	TOTAL	36		○ ○ △ ☐	
37		○ ○ △ ☐	TOTAL	37		○ ○ △ ☐	TOTAL

transportation are involved. It's important to remember, however, that in using a Flow Diagram, chart the flow of the person or item you are following. Be careful not to shift the study from the person to the item or vice versa.

Step 3.   Question Each Detail of the Job

Once you have completed the Flow Process Chart, study each detail listed and challenge it. This is the only way to discover what's wrong with the old method and how it can be improved. It requires an open and unbiased mind. It means you will have to decide what is opinion and what is fact. Work simplification is based on fact. A fact is something that doesn't disappear when you ask "Why?" Opinions are always hard to work with—they produce arguments. Facts are easy to work with — they produce conclusions.

Distinguish between causes and effects. When a job isn't going right, it's important to get at the cause. The effect is secondary. Take a broken fountain pen, for example. The fact that it is leaking is an effect, not a cause. Wearing rubber gloves, therefore, is not the real cure. The important thing is to fix the leak in the pen.

Don't be misled by an excuse if you're looking for a real reason. If a worker complains that wearing safety goggles gives him a headache, it may or may not be a real reason. Does he need prescription glasses? Has he had an eye examination? Is he over forty years of age? Is he just making up an excuse? These are questions to take into account.

When analyzing your Flow Process Chart, each detail must stand up under the following questions.

Write your answers on a sheet of paper. Don't worry if you get several answers to each one. At this point they are only possibilities from which to develop a better method.

a) *What is the purpose of the detail?* Why is it necessary? Does it do something? Can as good a result be obtained without it? If the detail adds no value or doesn't do what it's supposed to do, you can immediately question its necessity. Assume you're a supervisor in a department where the custom is to make four copies of every letter. Two copies are filed away and never referred to again. They serve no useful purpose. A wise move is to question the practice of making four copies in the first place.

b) *Where is the best place to do the detail?* If the detail is necessary, is it being done in the right place? If not, where should it be done? For many years, a milk chocolate firm in New York City sent three or four trucks to New England every few days for whole liquid-milk used in making chocolate. When the milk was delivered to the city, it first went to the company's dehydrating plant where it was turned into powdered milk. Eventually someone got the idea of moving the dehydrating equipment to New England. By dehydrating the milk on the spot where it was produced, the company found that only one truck was needed to carry the material back to the New York plant, whereas several trucks were needed before.

c) *When is the best time to do the detail?* Is it being done at the right time now? Should it be done at a different time? At the same time as some other detail? Before some other detail? After some other detail? For example, in one large department store clerks are required to fold boxes and set up counter displays. Supervisors found it more efficient to schedule such routine work for slow periods, thus leaving more time during the busy part of the day for attending to customers.

d) *Who should do the detail?* Is it being done by the right person now? Would it increase efficiency to have someone else do it? A good general rule to follow is to assign the lowest-paid worker who can do the job in a satisfactory manner. Not long ago a large university decided to save money by cutting down on the amount of student help hired to do clerical work in faculty and administrative offices. The university officials soon found that many well-paid professors and instructors were neglecting their classroom work because they were forced to spend much of their time doing routine tasks like addressing and mailing college bulletins. The university found it cheaper in the long run to rehire the student assistants at the pay they were getting before — seventy-five cents an hour.

e) *How should the detail be done?* Should you use a different tool or machine? Different materials? Can you improve your working conditions? Can you make the detail safer, more comfortable? Can you cut down on waste and wear and tear, both on men and equipment? How will the cost of making the product be affected? In a pearl button factory six girls were sorting thousands of buttons spread on a large table. They were grading them by color and imperfections. The old method on this detail was to pick the buttons up and drop them into a series of small boxes placed on the table. This method was improved by placing the boxes so that they were flush with the table top, thus enabling the girls to put fingers on the buttons and slide them into the proper box much the same as a bank teller counts silver. Production on this detail was tripled.

Step 4. Work Out a Better Method

After you've listed possible ways of improving each detail, you are ready to develop a better method. The first step is to be sure the entire job is still necessary. Would doing away with it result in a loss? Or would it increase efficiency?

Eliminating. Assuming the job is necessary, the next step is to eliminate as many details as possible. Examine your Flow Process Chart again and study the possibilities you have noted down. Investigate each detail of the job. Is it really necessary? Would doing away with it improve the job? Careful study and evaluation of this kind has led to many important technical improvements. Among these are the fountain pen, which eliminates inkwells; "windowpane" envelopes, which do away with the need to place names and addresses on the envelope itself; and carbon paper, which eliminates retyping copies.

One thing to keep in mind is that every job is made up of three parts:

a) *Make-Ready.* This is the effort and time put in setting up the equipment or the machine, or getting the material with which to work.

b) *Do.* This is the actual work done.

c) *Put-Away.* This is the clean-up process following the "Do."

You'll probably find that the biggest room for improvement is in getting rid of as much of the "Make-Ready" and "Put-Away" as is practical.

While studying your Flow Process Chart, it's also wise to pay special attention to details marked "Transportation" (o) or "Storage" (△). These two categories in most cases add no value to the final product. Eliminating as many of these details as possible will cut the final cost of producing the item and reduce the labor involved.

Combining. Wherever possible, the details now remaining should be combined. When two or more "operations" (O) are combined, they may sometimes be performed for the labor cost involved in only one operation. Combining also does away with transportation, storage, and unnecessary inspections between operations.

If operations cannot be combined, it may be possible for you to combine a transportation (o) with an operation (O). An example of this type of combination is the moving assembly line.

Changing the sequence. When there are no further ways of combining details, check to see if switching the sequence of remaining details will open the way for further improvement, particularly in cutting travel. In addition to your Flow Process Chart, a simple floor diagram of the job area, or Flow Diagram, will help bring out ways and means of making sequence changes.

Simplifying. By now it should be obvious that methods improvement and work simplification are one and the same thing. You'll note that the possibilities described — eliminating, combining, changing the sequence — are simply ways of cutting down the number of individual steps that complicate a job.

Even when you're down to the fewest possible details needed to do the job properly, the simplifying process does not end. Try to reduce even these steps to simplest terms. Economize on motion, effort, energy, and cost, keeping in mind the comfort and safety of the worker.

Motion economy. Simplifying at this stage involves applying principles of motion economy. Motion economy is a science utilizing our knowledge of the human body — muscles, nervous system, physical proportions, and the laws of gravity, leverage, momentum, etc. Here are some established rules that can be applied to almost any job:

1. *Let both hands do useful work.* Most of us have a tendency to work with one hand and use the other to hold objects. The hand is too valuable an instrument to be used as a holding device. Boxes, vises, clamps, hooks, jigs, fixtures, or other mechanical means can be utilized for this purpose.

Using both hands will often double output. In addition, it is less fatiguing. It is much less tiring to carry forty pounds of luggage in two twenty-pound suitcases than in one forty-pound suitcase.

Wherever possible, too, the hands should be relieved of all work that can be done by the feet. Many power-operated tools and machines use the principle of the foot pedal.

2. *Use "short transport" and few movements.* Tools and materials should be close to and directly in front of the worker so as to be within easy reach of the hands. Saving a few inches on a repeated motion by having "short transport" and as few movements as possible means saving miles of motion over a period of time.

3. *Pre-position tools and materials.* This means having an object in a definite and fixed place in such

a way that when needed it can be grasped in the position in which it will be used. The most common example of pre-positioning is the desk fountain pen set where the pen is held in writing position even when not in use. It can be quickly and easily removed or returned.

4. *Use "gravity feed" and "drop delivery."* We have all seen match containers that are hung on the kitchen wall and allow matches to drop down into position as they are required. The same principle used on the job saves time, effort, and strain. Bins and containers with sloping bottoms are known as "hoppers." They permit material to be fed by gravity and relieve the worker of having to dip down into the container to grasp or lift parts. In the same way, "drop delivery" allows the worker to dispose of finished items by dropping them into a chute which delivers them to their next destination. These methods have long been used by industrial companies, department stores, and the U. S. Post Office Department.

5. *Provide for sequence and rhythm.* Sequence means the arrangement of a series of parts, tools, or equipment. Rhythm results from introducing an "offbeat" into a repetitive job. Imagine, for example, a skilled typist striking away at the keys at high speed. She is repeatedly striking a series of pre-positioned keys. But as she reaches up every few moments and resets the typewriter carriage, she is introducing a different "note" and rhythm results. This relieves monotony and thus reduces fatigue.

Performing unnecessary motions is the mark of an inexperienced or unskilled worker. As he becomes more skilled, he eliminates most of these wasted motions; that is, he unlearns the waste motions. When he becomes superskilled, he introduces an easy and natural rhythm whether he realizes it or not.

Sequence and rhythm are essential to the smooth and semiautomatic performance of an operation The worker should have a chance to introduce them in his job.

6. *Consider the worker's comfort and health.* If possible, the height of the workbench and chairs should be adjustable and permit alternate sitting and standing at work. Allowing the worker to vary his position enables him to rest certain sets of muscles. Also, a change of position improves circulation. Sitting or standing for long periods of time produces fatigue. In many kinds of work, arrangements can easily be made for this sitting-standing combination, and some states have laws requiring workplaces to be planned with this in mind. Chairs designed for good posture and individual adjustment are also important for health and comfort.

Lighting must be planned according to work requirements. Errors, accidents, fatigue, and morale may be affected if the light is too strong, too weak, the wrong color, glaring, or beamed in the wrong direction. Color harmony and three dimensional painting have a good effect on morale and productivity.

Step 5. *Put the New Method to Work*

You probably know the old saying: "Good ideas are a dime a dozen." Putting them to work is the tough part. This is particularly true of ideas on improving methods.

Putting a new method into effect calls for the same careful planning and work that went into figuring out the method itself. There are two major obstacles to deal with. These are the technical problem and the human problem.

The Technical Problem. Of concern here are the questions: How practical is the new method? Will it work? Will it save money?

Write up the new method so that you yourself are clear on every detail. You can best do this by filling in the new method Flow Process Chart or Flow Diagram. List every detail, just as you did earlier with the old method. This will give you a complete written record which you or others can evaluate.

Next, study the breakdown of the new method and decide objectively the probable over-all cost of installing the new method. Will there be any financial benefit in making the change? Can it be started with equipment and material already on hand? Or will it require a lot of new machines and materials that are expensive and hard to obtain? A point to bear in mind is that if you spend some time looking around the plant, and look hard enough, you will probably find that most of what is needed is already available. If you conclude that the technical problems can be overcome, write down a careful estimate of the quantities, quality, tooling, designs, forms, and time required to put the new method into effect.

The Human Problem. You are now ready to begin "selling" your idea. The best product or system in the world has to be sold to the consumer or user before it can be put into use. In putting the new method into effect, you have to take over the role of salesman. You have to sell the new method to the people above you and to the workers under you.

Selling the "Boss"

Your boss is not interested in half-baked plans or long-winded explanations. He wants to know exactly what the new method is and what it will accomplish. He wants specific figures on what it will save in dollars or man-hours, what it will cost to install the improved system, and how long it will take before benefits are received from it. Your boss is concerned not only with the method itself but whether it can be put into effect.

This means that you will have to get him to give you enough time for a detailed and factual explanation. Since bosses are usually busy people, your best approach is to submit a written memo describing your idea. This memo acts as a "teaser" and also helps you to organize your own thinking.

What form should the memo take? It should be as brief as possible. Keep it free of involved and complicated details, and don't waste words criticizing the present method. You might begin it by pointing out clearly and simply why a new method is needed. Perhaps there is a bottleneck. Perhaps production is lower than normal. Perhaps quality can be improved.

Outline briefly the major points in your new method. List exactly how it will increase production, improve quality, control accidents, boost morale, make more efficient use of man-hours, or cut costs. If the new method can be put into effect largely by using equipment and material already on hand, stress this fact.

You might point out near the end of the memo that the change will more than pay for itself within a specified period — say three to six months — and that you have data to prove it. In the concluding paragraph, request the boss to let you know when you might discuss your suggestions with him.

It's hard for any executive to disregard this type of memo. Be prepared when you're called in for a talk. Have your facts lined up. In addition to the Flow Process Chart, bring along any sketches, samples, diagrams, or models that will help make a dramatic presentation.

Many supervisors fail in selling the boss on a new method because they concentrate on the past instead of the future. They spend most of the discussion period telling the boss why the old system is no good. Since, as we already pointed out, people resent criticism, the boss doesn't like to be told that the method he's been using all along — a system he himself may have introduced — is wrong. Don't tear down the old method in order to build up the new. Concentrate on a positive presentation. Spend most of your time discussing the merits of your own improved method.

Every method, of course, has some weaknesses. And this includes your own. It's a good idea to bring these weaknesses to your boss's attention before he mentions them. You probably won't like to admit them. But the boss will be more receptive if he feels you're trying to be as objective as possible.

Also bear in mind that no matter how objective you are, there may be factors the boss is aware of that you're not. He has to look at the over-all picture. Although your plan may be excellent, it may not be practical at the present time. But even if it is turned down, don't assume that the time and effort you spent was a complete loss. It is always proper to revise and submit your improved method at a later and more suitable time. Not only do you still have the plan available for future use, but you will have learned about "angles" that you hadn't known about or considered before. And the boss won't forget that he has a supervisor on his staff who is ambitious, helpful and not afraid to do some original thinking.

Selling the Worker.

Assuming your new method has been approved, there still remains the task of selling the idea to the workers affected. This is often even more important than selling the boss.

Every time a new way of doing things is introduced, some workers are affected. It is understandable, therefore, that they are vitally concerned with your new method. If nothing is done to prepare them for the change, they may be hostile and refuse to cooperate. They may think of the improved method in terms of old-style "efficiency engineering" and look upon it as a threat to their job security. Added to this is the normal resentment of criticism and resistance to change that is present in all of us. Your new system may be doomed even before it is put into operation.

It was pointed out earlier in this chapter, however, that modern work simplification takes into account the human factor. It seeks to make improvements with the worker's knowledge and cooperation, not at his expense.

What steps should you follow? The most important is to take the workers into your confidence before the improved method goes into effect. The earlier they know what you are planning, the more time they'll have to think about it calmly and intelligently. The change-over will seem less drastic.

It's a good idea to let workers know of your new method before you submit the plan to the boss. Discuss it with them. Invite them to contribute their ideas and suggestions. The method will thus receive the benefit of being reviewed and checked by many heads instead of only one. The workers will look upon it as partly their own and will want to see it work successfully.

What if they express fear that it may eliminate jobs? It's up to you to demonstrate that it won't do that at all. Outline the method step by step and show them how it will make their jobs easier and safer; how it will increase production, lower costs, and eventually create even more jobs. If necessary, explain frankly that while some retraining and reassignment may be made, no one will lose his job. Be sure your company is behind this essential policy.

It is wise to give the improved method a trial run before putting it into operation. Request the cooperation of the workers. The test will show whether the new system actually works and will help iron out unexpected kinks. It will also show the workers how the change-over is to be made and thus insures against sudden changes in routine later on. If the plan is in effect at another company, check up and include this evidence in your presentation.

Once the new method is in regular operation, see to it that all those who participated receive full credit for their efforts and contributions. Giving a worker deserved recognition means much to him and assures you of his future cooperation and loyalty.

Follow up the improvement. After the system has been introduced, frequent checkups are necessary since it is easy to revert to old ways without even realizing it. Make sure that the full benefits outlined in the original plans are actually being received. If not, find out why. And don't overlook safety regulations, especially while the worker is learning the new method and is bound to make some mistakes. See if the improved system can be applied to other jobs as well. Keep an open mind and don't assume that your way is the final and "best" way. Be receptive to ideas submitted by others on how your "baby" can be improved even further. Remember that an open mind and constant effort are the two basic requirements for continuing to discover the "best" and easiest way of doing things.

EIGHT

HOW TO SOLVE A PROBLEM

In supervision, as in anything else, the best way to handle a problem is to prevent it. One way to do this is to carry out as perfectly as possible the various phases of your supervisory job described in the previous chapters. By concentrating on building employee morale, winning cooperation, reducing accidents and injuries, improving work methods, and giving job instructions properly, your problems will automatically be reduced to a minimum.

There is no such thing as absolute perfection where human beings are concerned. You make mistakes occasionally. So do the men and women you supervise, and so do your superiors. Tools and machines break down at times. Shortages of material, lack of manpower, and drops in consumer demand are unforseeable factors that may arise.

Inasmuch as such conditions cannot always be planned for in advance, you meet up with a certain number of problems. If you've carried out the other phases of your job well, these problems will undoubtedly be few and far between. But they will have to be solved if you expect to succeed as a supervisor. Even little problems, if neglected, often snowball into major ones.

How should you handle a problem when it does come up? Whether the problem is small or large, there are four basic steps you can take in order to reach the best solution. These are:

1. Defining the problem
2. Estimating the situation
3. Taking action
4. Examining the results

There is nothing new or mysterious about this procedure. Nor it is confined to solving problems of supervision alone. This process, or a very similar one, is used in almost every field of endeavor. Scientists, faced with a research problem in the laboratory, use the "Scientific Method" to solve it. Army and Navy officers, in solving military problems, refer to the procedure as the "Estimate of the Situation." Engineers solve problems by use of the "Engineering Approach." The pattern of thinking involved in problem-solving is virtually the same in each case.

What happens when you visit your physician because you have a pain in your chest? Since you are dumping a problem in his lap, the first thing he does is to *define it*. He wants to know whether the pain is real or imagined; whether it is caused by a physical or a mental condition; how often and exactly where the pain is felt. He notes down facts about your past illnesses and family background, and makes a thorough examination of your present physical condition. This information, which enables him to define what the problem is, is called the case history.

Once all the known facts are at his finger tips, the physician proceeds with a diagnosis and prescription. This is equivalent to the second step in handling a problem — *estimating the situation*. By examining your case history, the physician can usually diagnose what's wrong with you. Then he considers several possible courses of action. The one he finally chooses must be practical as well as helpful.

Perhaps the doctor feels the problem is too complicated for him to handle. He may prescribe a visit to a specialist. Or he concludes that a few weeks of complete rest will clear up the trouble. Among the courses of action he might weigh are: 1) the use of drugs; 2) a trip to Florida or a rest cure in a sanitarium; 3) several weeks in bed at home; 4) have you follow your regular routine.

Among the questions the physician asks himself to reach a practical as well as a helpful solution are: Are you allergic to the drugs? Can you afford a vacation or a stay at a rest home? If you remain at home, will you get the care and attention you need? Would continuing on the job aggravate your condition?

Once the physician gives you his final prescription, and you follow it, the problem has entered the *taking action* phase. When this step is completed, you return to the physician to see if the action did any good. This is the *examining the results* stage. The doctor may give you another medical checkup and compare his new findings with the case history he drew up at the beginning. This enables him to see if the problem has cleared up, or to decide what else must be done. It also gives him an opportunity to complete his record of your case for reference purposes if you return at a later date or if he meets up with a similar problem in the future.

Your supervisory problems may be different than those of a physician, but your approach in handling them should be the same. Supervisory problems fall into two categories — personnel and technical. Personnel problems include worker tardiness, absenteeism, poor job performance, improper employee attitudes, etc. Technical problems involve such situations as breakdown of equipment, shortage of materials, lack of transportation. Problems usually involve both personnel and technical aspects.

Solving supervisory problems calls for the same objective and unemotional approach as that used by a physician. You must fix your attention on one problem at a time and solve it before tackling others. Flitting from problem to problem without investigating or acting intensively on any one simply results in more numerous and more complex problems. Let's examine in detail the four basic steps in handling a problem.

1. DEFINING THE PROBLEM

The first step in handling any problem is to decide what the problem is. Attempting to reach a solution without first defining what it is you're trying to solve is futile. The result is a waste of time, thought, and effort. Often, with a bit of careful investigation, what was believed to be a major problem turns out to be a minor one. Other times a situation that on the surface appears simple and easy to handle is found to be more serious.

Suppose your car stalls suddenly on a highway miles from a service station. Your first move is to find out what the problem is. You may ask yourself, "Do I need gas?" If so, your problem is to thumb a ride to the nearest filling station. If this were not the case, you would probably wonder:

"Can I make an easy on-the-spot mechanical adjustment myself? Is the breakdown so serious that my problem is how to get a mechanic or have the car towed to a repair shop?

The only way you can decide what the problem is, is by carefully collecting the facts. The more facts you get the better your possibilities of solving the problem. Like the physician mentioned earlier you cannot solve it without a "case history." Preconceived notions, misinformation, and half-facts are not keys to a real solution. You must assume at the beginning that you don't know the whole story. If you already knew all the facts, the chances are that the problem would not be there in the first place. Charles Kettering, the famous automobile research wizard, once said: "It ain't the things you don't know that'll get you in trouble, but the things you know for sure that ain't so."

Executives often complain that most difficult problems referred to them by supervisors are "tough" only because the supervisor found them to be tough before getting all the facts. Reports of such problems lack vital points of information which, if obtained in the beginning, would have reduced the problems to simple ones that could have been solved by the supervisor himself.

How can you get the facts? By personal observation, by interviewing employees, and by checking company rules.

Personal Observation

This requires legwork and honest digging for information. Visit the problem spot yourself to see what's going on. This is especially important in the case of technical problems — those involving machine breakdowns, material shortages, etc. Don't be content with what you yourself think is the situation. Go right to where the problem is and take a long look at it. Is it as bad as you've been led to believe? It is worse? Note down in writing the facts you've found. Describe the picture as completely as possible. List surrounding conditions, even though they may seem remote to the actual problem at the present time. Take your time! A half-baked solution based on incomplete or hurriedly-gathered facts is more costly and time-consuming in the long run than a real solution based on complete, up-to-date information. Other supervisors may have valuable information pertaining to your problem.

The Interview

Much of your "case history" will have to be based on what you learn from the men and women you supervise. This is particularly true where personnel problems are concerned. Adopting a closed-door policy and discouraging complaints will not get you the facts. Nor will you learn of problems that you weren't aware of before if you adopt a hear-no-evil, see-no-evil attitude. Sooner or later you will have to meet a problem head on. And it may have grown to critical proportions.

During the fact-gathering talks that take place in interviews, problems often disappear by themselves. The reason is that many times a problem exists only in an employee's mind or because he has false or incomplete information. Although the problem may seem trivial or nonexistent to you, it is real enough

for the employee concerned. Regardless of what
you yourself think, the opinions and feelings of those
under you, whether right or wrong, have to be dealt
with. They are very important to the person or persons involved. By listening with patience and sympathy, by weighing the facts, and by explaining the
situation as it actually exists, you can usually solve
a problem that might become serious if ignored.
Learn to be a good listener. "Talk it out." It is one
of the best ways to clear up misunderstandings.

Many supervisors don't bother to listen. This is
one of the most common complaints employees have
against their bosses. Frequently a supervisor forgets
that the real purpose of a fact-gathering interview
is to get the facts. Instead, he turns it into a long-
winded lecture or a trial in which the worker is the
defendant.

When interviewing employees who come to you
with a problem, it is always a good idea to start the
ball rolling with a pleasant smile. An interview can
be informative and pleasant, or it can be an ordeal.
It depends on how you approach it. You might begin by asking a question or two to break the ice. But
once the worker begins to talk, don't interrupt unless it's necessary. It's foolish to try to figure out for
yourself what an employee has on his mind when
you can find out directly by listening to him. Don't
browbeat, accuse, or criticize. Belligerence discour-
ages frankness. Your purpose at this point is to get
information, not to sit in judgment.

Very often a single fact is sufficient to change the
whole complexion of a problem. For example:

A supervisor in a large eastern food plant noticed
that one of his men punched in late on Monday

mornings. A talk with the employee revealed that his tardiness was due to "too much celebrating" on week ends. After several additional latenesses and warnings, the supervisor lost patience. He gave the worker an ultimatum: Either get in on time or be suspended. The employee realized that the supervisor meant business. He promised not to let it happen again.

The following Monday the worker showed up thirty minutes late. The supervisor immediately strode over. "Okay," he said angrily, "you've asked for it. Take the rest of the week off!"

The employee tried to reason, but his explanation fell on deaf ears. "I don't want to hear what you have to say," interrupted the supervisor. "You can't talk me out of anything this time."

Reluctantly the suspended worker picked up his lunch box and left the plant.

The supervisor sensed that the other men and women in his department were angry and resentful. It wasn't until he accidently learned the entire story from another supervisor that he understood why.

The worker he'd suspended had been late this time not because of "too much celebrating" but because he had been in an automobile accident while on his way to work. In his anxiety to get to work on time the employee even refused to go to a nearby doctor to be examined for possible injuries.

Checking Company Rules

To complete your case history, also check on company rules and policy. Find out if your problem is covered by existing regulations. If it isn't, investigate whether similar cases have arisen in the past.

Knowing how the problem was handled before will aid you in reaching a solution. Here's an illustration:

Suppose you are a supervisor in a company where hiring for your department is left up to you. One of your men requests that you employ his brother. The brother is a skilled worker, and you'd like to hire him. But you're afraid that having two members of the same family in your department might lead to resentment among the other workers.

The proper procedure is to check on company policy. Do company rules specifically forbid this type of arrangement? Have there been other instances? How did they work out? The answers to these questions should be obtained in order to arrive at an intelligent and workable solution.

2.   Estimating the Situation

Once you have defined the problem and completed your case history, you are ready for the next step — *estimating the situation*. Examine the facts, weigh them, draw up possible solutions. Your task is similar to that of fitting together a jigsaw puzzle. The facts are like pieces of the puzzle. You have to select those that are related and group them together. Arranging a clear picture of the problem calls for judgment as to which facts are related and which are not. And your decisions must be based on the relationship and importance of the facts at the present time.

Let's go back to the case where you are asked by an employee to hire his brother. We'll assume that certain facts indicate it wouldn't be a good idea to have two brothers working in the same department. Yet it may also be that the company is facing a serious labor shortage, and skilled workers are next to impossible to find. This fact might carry a great deal of weight — perhaps enough to outweigh the unfavorable aspects.

Consider the problem of absenteeism. What action should you take if a number of workers stay out without giving satisfactory reasons? There is no single solution. If the absenteeism takes place during a "slow" period, you might feel that drastic action is not required. But you have to take immediate action if it occurs when your department is faced with a huge backlog of orders. The when-it-happens factor is very important.

Develop More than One Solution

If you have examined, arranged, and weighed the facts carefully, you are ready to develop possible answers to the problem Draw up at least three solutions incorporating ideas of your subordinates and of other supervisors.

The reason for more than one solution is important, yet often overlooked. The first solution you develop is apt to be the most obvious one. But the obvious decision is not necessarily the best. Approach your problem from all angles and develop other solutions. You may find answers which were not apparent in the beginning and which best meet your problem.

Don't look for extreme or oversimplified answers only. Many supervisors tend to view extreme measures as the only possible courses of action. They overlook completely the "middle-ground" approach

Remember, problems involving human beings are not usually simple. Answers cannot always be in simple black-and-white terms. Few solutions are perfect and entirely satisfactory to everyone.

Keep this principle in mind when selecting the final choice from your possible solutions. Here, again, you'll find that real solutions often rest on compromise. It may turn out that the best solution is one that is actually a combination of two or more.

Evaluate in your own mind how each possible decision on your list would affect the individual, the group, production and service.

The answer to a supervisory problem can be compared to a three-legged stool. If your solution is sound, it should rest on the above three interests in such a way as to strike a reasonable balance.

You must estimate the effect of the decision on each factor as fairly as possible. These interests don't always coincide. A solution that satisfies one may not serve the other two at all. Such a lopsided solution is not satisfactory. A sound solution should enable you to give reasonably acceptable answers when you ask yourself these three questions: How will it affect the individual involved? How will it affect the group? How will it affect production or service? If the solution doesn't satisfy these test questions, the chances are it is not a real answer.

3.   TAKING ACTION

Supervisors who are unsuccessful in solving problems generally fall into one of two types.

There is the "hasty action" supervisor who makes the mistake of thinking that action alone is the key to a problem. He is so anxious to do something that he plunges into the *taking action* step without first bothering to define the problem or estimate the situation. And he usually comes up with the wrong answer. He ends up thinking the problem out afterwards. Then he must not only give thought to the original problem but also to the question of how to undo the additional damage his hasty "solution" may have caused.

The second is the "pipe-smoking philosopher" type of supervisor. Even after he has several possible solutions, this supervisor continues to drag out the deliberation process. He becomes bogged down trying to decide which solution to choose because of trifling differences between them. The result is that either he never reaches the *taking action* phase or else he reaches it so late that the decision is now of little value. He doesn't realize that taking prompt action on any one solution is better than putting off all the solutions. Delaying the *taking action* step too often may become a habit with this type of supervisor. Postponing decisions rather than actually solving problems becomes his real goal.

Problem-solving requires *deliberation* (defining the problem and estimating the situation) followed by *decisive* activity (taking action and examining the results). It can be likened to the behavior of a cat who, after quietly stalking its prey and observing it from all directions, finally pounces on it.

Consult Others

Consult others after you have decided on the final solution. It's a good idea to pause for a moment and ask yourself: "Should I go ahead under my own steam and put it into action? Should I consult with my boss?" At this stage you are like the physician who must decide whether to trust his own diagnosis and prescription, or to call in a specialist.

There are several reasons why you may want to talk over the problem with your superior. After studying the situation from every angle, you may still be uncertain about the best solution. Or perhaps the problem and decision are major ones affecting the company as a whole, in which case you wonder whether you have the right to take the necessary action on your own.

You don't want to call in your boss on every little problem. But if the problem is difficult, big, or new, you would be wise to seek his aid. His job is to help you in just such situations and no one has ever lost face by admitting that he doesn't know all the answers. Your superior can advise you and can consult with other executives. If there is a question as to who has the authority to take the action, he will know or at least know how to find out.

Here are five rules to follow when consulting the boss or others on a problem. These rules will save your time as well as his and will also convince him that you have a sound grasp of the situation.

a) Be sure you understand the problem thoroughly and have all the known facts to present.

b) Give him your solution and explain exactly how you think it will help the situation.

c) Listen to his suggestions.

d) Weigh his suggestions. Agree or disagree, giving your honest opinion. If there is a sharp difference, and you are firmly convinced you are on the right track, see if a compromise can be reached.

e) Make certain he understands and gives his approval to the final plan of action.

Even when a problem doesn't require consulting with the boss beforehand, it's important at least to inform him and others of the action you're taking. This is frequently overlooked. Yet it's necessary if you want to make certain that what you're doing will mesh with their actions. A company is like a huge machine — making changes in one part of the company machine may affect other parts all along the line.

In addition to informing your boss, let other supervisors know of your decision. This will give them a chance to make adjustments in their operations, if necessary. It may also help them profit by your experience in case they are faced with a similar problem in the future.

Select the Proper Time

Timing is a vital factor when you take action on a problem. You've figured out *how* it should be done. Now you must decide *when* to do it. Should you do it today? Tomorrow? Next week? Perfectly good decisions fail because they are executed at the wrong time. We have all heard the expression, "Timing is just right." Problem-solving requires you to apply this principle constantly. Factors that determine the proper time may include such things as government regulations, weather, season activities.

Take the problem of trying to get a raise. Everyone knows it is foolish to approach the boss when he's angry, worried, or tied up with other matters.

Consider the case of an office manager faced with the problem of reorganizing the office files, a major job. When should he do it? Obviously he should schedule it for a time when it won't interfere with work that has to be attended to immediately.

Work through People

Most problems arise because of some human weakness, failure, blind spot, or oversight. This means that in solving them you usually have to work with people — your boss, the men and women under you, or supervisors of other departments. Unless they're willing to cooperate, your decision will not be carried out successfully. A solution that can't be put into operation is not really a solution at all.

How do you get people to cooperate in solving a problem? Explain the situation fully. Let them know about the nature of the problem. Tell them why it must be licked. Show them how they, personally, are affected while the trouble remains. Go over the problem in detail. Invite their opinions and suggestions for solving it. You can't expect them to be enthusiastic about shouldering responsibility unless they also feel they have a stake in the decision and the outcome.

If the solution calls for the cooperation or help of other supervisors, don't bypass them under the theory that you'll save time and trouble. There are no short cuts where human feelings are involved. They may get the impression you're trying to hog credit or go over their heads. The result is likely to be resentment, rivalry, and lack of cooperation in the future.

Once you put the solution into action, be prepared to stand behind it. Don't pass the buck if it doesn't work out. Just because you may have consulted with your superior or others doesn't relieve you of responsibility. Basically the decision is yours.

Dodging responsibility, if the course of action is disagreeable or doesn't turn out well, is always poor policy. Never tell a worker, "I would like to have done something else, but the boss wouldn't let me." The only thing you'll win by such an excuse is the disrespect of all concerned. Employees will condemn you for being too weak to stand up for your own rights as well as theirs. And your superior, if he hears about it, will lose his respect for your integrity.

4. EXAMINING THE RESULTS

Up to this point your solution is still unproved. You've figured out in theory how it should work. Now you must observe it in operation to see if it actually does work. You can only do this by examining the results carefully. Look for changes in the attitude, relationship, or output of individual employees concerned. Try to gauge the effect on the rest of the group. What is the general reaction? Examine the quality and quantity of production. Has it improved, fallen off, or remained the same?

Refer back to your original case history. Compare the situation then with what it is now. Have the symptoms that tipped you off to the problem in the first place disappeared? Has the solution to this one problem led to other changes — changes that might be symptoms of new problems?

If your solution isn't working out as well as you thought, think about what changes or adjustments might be needed. Don't be afraid to make them. A course of action rarely works as well in practice as it does on paper. There are usually "bugs" that have to be ironed out. If an examination of the results show a need for adjustment, it's a mistake to stick like glue to your original plan simply out of stubbornness or a false sense of pride.

It's also helpful to check up on yourself at this point. Do you feel that you handled the problem in the best possible manner? Were there things you would do differently the next time? Complete your case history by making notes for use in handling similar situations in the future. If you have the time you might even want to write up the problem and how you handled it.

If examining the results indicates that you have hit upon an unusually effective solution, you'll want to report it to your fellow supervisors and to your boss. Your boss, in turn, will want to pass it on to other executives who may be up against similar problems.

Problem-Solving Isn't Simple

Handling problems is one of your toughest but most important and rewarding jobs as a supervisor. It's tough because in most cases you will be dealing with people, and getting people to cooperate for a common cause is not an easy task. It's important because problems are obstacles to smooth operation. They waste time; they hurt efficiency; they increase costs; they can mar your record and that of your department unless you handle them properly.

Perhaps many of the points discussed here seem to be simple, obvious, and nothing but common sense.

Yet there is an old saying: "There's nothing as uncommon as common sense." Not only many supervisors, but men and women in every field, find themselves continually bogged down with problems they can't solve. Does this mean the problems have no solution? Not at all. It means that too many of us have gotten into the habit of short-circuiting our thinking processes. We just don't take the time and effort to think a problem through.

This is a serious mistake. It causes failure not only in supervision, but in daily life. It is the reason why many of us fail as people, especially today when we are faced with tension and indecision in almost every phase of living.

The difference between success and failure in every walk of life is that the successful person has trained himself to handle his problems. The unsuccessful man or woman doesn't know how to deal with the difficulties that beset him from day to day. He is constantly tense and indecisive. The earmark of a good supervisor or executive is his ability to achieve sound, acceptable solutions to a good percentage of his problems.

You may have noticed that this chapter did not give specific answers to specific problems. This was done purposely. The reason is that only you are in a position to develop solutions to the problems that face you. Only you have a close knowledge of the men and women you work with; only you know the personality of the executives over you; only you know exactly how your company operates; only you understand the situation in your department.

Instead of giving you specific answers, the real purpose of this chapter was to describe a "process of thought" that can serve you as a guide in handling any problem. You may find that this method is clumsy at first because it's new to you and different from what you have done in the past. But when you apply it you'll find yourself handling problems more rapidly. You will begin to use this method through habit; you will apply it almost automatically to personal as well as to supervisory problems. This way of thinking will become a part of your personality. It will help you beget the loyalty, respect, and co-operation of those who work with you. In addition to adding to your ability to get things done, it will also help you win that most important of all prizes — greater peace of mind.

CHECK LIST

How To Solve A Problem

Define the Problem
1. Get the background.
2. Observe the situation.
3. Talk with all the people involved.
4. Consider opinions and feelings as facts that have to be dealt with.
5. Decide exactly what the problem is.

Estimate the Situation
1. Arrange the information.
2. Fit the facts together.
3. Develop at least three solutions.
4. Consider the effect of each solution on the individual, on the group, on production and on service.
5. Select your final solution.

Take Action
1. Consult with your boss if you need help.
2. Determine the best time for action.
3. Discuss the problem and solution with those who may help you.
4. Work with and through others.

Examine the Results
1. Watch for changes in individual attitude, group reaction, and output.
2. Compare the situation now with what it was at the beginning.
3. Make adjustments as necessary.
4. Ask yourself what you have learned.
5. Keep a record.
6. Pass on your findings to others.

NINE

THE SUPERVISOR AS A MANAGER

THE BASIC MEANING OF THE WORD "MANAGE" is to carry out, guide, direct, and use means to accomplish an end or purpose. The supervisor doesn't make company rules or policies. He carries out the plans of top management. In this sense he is a true manager. Many companies have recognized this fact and have begun to refer to supervisors as "managers." As our nation's business and industrial organizations have grown in size and become more and more affected by federal and state laws and union agreements, the supervisor's functions as a manager have mushroomed. Since each industry and company has its own individual problems, it is not possible for a book on the general subject of supervision to cover every specific function of supervisors in hundreds of different industries and thousands of different plants. In this chapter we will try to describe briefly some of the more common managerial situations and problems that supervisors meet.

THE NEWLY-PROMOTED SUPERVISOR

The newly-promoted foreman or supervisor faces a number of problems. For one thing, he must change his thinking and attitude. Since he was a worker himself not so long ago, this isn't always easy.

He may find it difficult to realize he is now a representative of management. He can't help but feel a sense of loyalty to those who used to be his fellow-workers. He may be worried that his feeling of loyalty will conflict with his duties as a supervisor. He is especially worried about what he will do when problems of discipline arise.

A good supervisor learns to overcome this situation. He does it by combining fairness with firmness. He balances his loyalty to his men with a sense of responsibility to management. He guards equally the rights of employees and the rights of management.

THE SUPERVISOR — HIS "BOSS" AND HIS WORKERS

If a supervisor is ambitious for quick promotions, he may be tempted to ignore or neglect the welfare of his workers and spend most of his time and effort trying to please his boss, the department head, or plant manager. Such a supervisor is said to be "bucking," to use one expression for it. His reputation spreads quickly throughout the average company, and stories about him usually reach top management. Invariably this situation causes low morale and resentment among his men who feel they cannot depend on him to stand up for them. Efficiency suffers and disciplinary problems begin to arise.

The supervisor who "bucks" fails to realize that he is judged by the results he achieves in dealing with the employees under him. If production falls off and absenteeism or other morale problems occur too often, it doesn't matter how hard he tries to please his superior's vanity. He is looked upon as a poor leader because he isn't getting results. He stands little chance of being considered for promotion because in the eyes of company executives, and also of the workers, he has been marked as a "talker" instead of a "doer."

The supervisor who protects the rights of the men under him, and gets them to give their best efforts, shows that he takes his responsibilities seriously. He is respected for his independence not only by those under him, but by top management; and he is considered a good choice for promotion to a job calling for even greater responsibility. A good rule-of-thumb policy for the supervisor to follow is to spend 90 per cent of his time and effort working with the men under him and thinking about their problems, and about 10 per cent trying to do what he thinks will look good to his superior.

RELATIONS WITH OTHER SUPERVISORS

Often because of rivalry and lack of understanding, a supervisor may want to be the "star" of the company team. He may begin to wear mental "horse-blinders." Instead of seeing the work of his department as one part of the over-all company operation, he sees it as an independent operation. Let's say one supervisor requests the foreman of another group to lend him some men to break a bottleneck that is holding up company production. Unless ordered to do so from "above," the second supervisor may refuse. After all, why should he fall behind in his own production to help out a supervisor who may be a rival for promotion if a better job opens up?

What this supervisor doesn't realize, of course, is that his success is judged not only by what his particular department does. Top management, whose function it is to see company operation as a whole, sees this supervisor's department as only one of many in the company setup. And because top management is primarily interested in the final product, it is definitely concerned with how a supervisor cooperates with other departments.

The successful supervisor doesn't put blinders on himself. He sees his job as one in which he must constantly ask himself, "How can I best serve the interest of the company as a whole?"

Today American companies are larger and more complicated than ever before. The heads of these firms are aware that getting supervisors to work together is a major problem. One solution being used successfully is to call supervisors and foremen together for conferences at regular intervals. Though called for the purpose of discussing new policies or improved production methods, the meetings also serve as an opportunity for supervisors to become better acquainted and to get to know each other better. When one supervisor knows what the foreman in another department is thinking and what his individual problems are, there is a good chance that there will be less friction and greater cooperation between these two in the future.

Some supervisory types. How and why a person acts as he does is still open to question, although some psychologists claim to have the answer. What we do know is that few of us act in exactly the same way all the time. Almost every human being has a number of "faces." He shows one face to his wife, another to his friends, a third to his co-workers, and so on. Each of these faces changes from time to time, depending on circumstances. One evening the wife will suggest a movie, and the husband will agree, thinking it is a fine idea. Another time she will suggest taking in a movie and he will refuse because he is "not in the mood." It is hard to predict what a person's thoughts and actions will be at any given time. Experts who take scientific public opinion polls are aware of this. They have become cautious about making predictions, having been proved wrong in the past.

Almost everyone has his good and his bad traits. Which ones he shows at a certain time depend on a great many circumstances at the moment. We are likely to be charitable one day and selfish the next; cross in the morning and happy in the afternoon. There are always a few people, of course, who seem to be more set in their habits and actions than the rest of us.

How does this apply to the supervisor? There is a temptation for the worker to classify his supervisor according to one of a number of commonly-accepted "boss types." Unfortunately, too, it is a human habit to concentrate on a person's bad traits and overlook his good ones. The result is that the supervisor who has been "typed" is usually labeled because of his bad habits rather than his good qualities. He may not entirely deserve his poor reputation, but it can be damaging all the same because once he is typed it is difficult for him to overcome it. Like most human beings, a worker hates to have to admit, even to himself, that he has made a mistake. He will resist changing his initial impression as much as possible.

There are five commonly-accepted types of "bad bosses" that workers recognize. The supervisor should examine his own thinking and actions carefully to avoid even giving the impression that he falls into one of these categories:

The "slave-driver." The slave-driving supervisor pushes his workers as long and as hard as possible. He regards them as machines; he sees no point in employing mechanical aids or other devices to make their job easier or more comfortable. His answer to the question of how to increase productive efficiency is to drive the employees even harder. The growth of unions and progressive management thinking has made this type of boss less common. Today most companies know that management-worker relations must be based on persuasion, not on fear; that supervisors must be leaders, not drivers.

The "jelly-fish." The jelly-fish type of boss is inconsistent, indecisive, and contradictory. His main trouble is that he is uncertain of himself, of his knowledge of the details of his job, and of his ability to handle people. Because he wants to be popular with his men and superiors, he is like a straw in the wind, yielding to the latest pressure. He never inspires loyalty or respect. His workers consider that taking advantage of him is an interesting game. The result is that he becomes angry and irritated. When enough anger and irritation have been stored up, he "blows off steam," usually when he is in the wrong again. Then the same cycle begins anew. Although he tries his best to please, he never seems to please at all.

The "politician." The supervisor who "plays politics" wears a coat of many colors. He tells one thing to his superiors and another to his men. He also changes each story from time to time as it suits his convenience. A handy weapon he uses is to pit one employee against another. The company's welfare is always secondary to his own desire for personal gain. Usually a smooth and fast talker, he is adept at covering errors and equally skillful at "passing the buck" or finding someone else to bear the blame for his mistakes.

The "confused" supervisor. As the name implies, the confused supervisor doesn't fully understand what his job calls for. He may be a skilled workman or a trained technician. In fact the confused supervisor is quite common among highly educated scientific workers. Yet, he never realizes that his main job is to get others to do the actual work.

This type of supervisor would rather use his hands than his head because he is afraid the "big boss" will think he is loafing if he doesn't look busy. He pays more attention to getting the work out with his own effort than to the direction of the ten or twenty subordinates who have been provided to do the job.

The "bustler." Ambition and a desire for recognition and praise are traits that are present in all of us. But with the "bustler," it is a disease. He is so driven by ambition and a desire for self-importance that nothing else matters. He orders his men to consult him on every detail. Ideas developed by them are criticized and discarded for the present. Later they are "adopted" by him and passed off as his own. He always looks busy. If he has an office, he keeps visitors waiting because he thinks it adds to his self-importance. He chooses his friends carefully, making certain they are all on his own supervisory level or above him. To his subordinates, on the other hand, he is exceptionally formal, aloof, and at times rude.

DEVELOPING SUBORDINATES

Among other benefits, developing subordinates is an activity that boosts morale tremendously. When you have a "stand in," your job is covered in case you are ill, absent for business reasons, or on vacation. It is a way of rewarding the employee who does good work and of encouraging others to try harder. It builds employee respect because workers like a boss who isn't afraid of competition. It frees you for further promotions by eliminating the fear of top management that there's no one in your department to take over your job.

How should you select an understudy? Many managers feel there is no standard set of personality qualifications that can be used in picking out good supervisory material. An employee with a strong personality may or may not make a good supervisor. The same is true of the worker with a good-natured, easygoing disposition. By the same token, it is unfair to rule out the highstrung, emotional employee as good supervisory material. One top management executive explains: "If we were to do a complete job of screening out all emotional supervisors, we'd get people who are normal in every respect, but we'd be eliminating the type of individual who helped to give us electric power, television, lifesaving drugs, and most of the other benefits mankind now has. We'd be screening out men and women with the drive needed to make a company progress."

One reason why personality traits are not an accurate guide to choosing potential supervisors is that most employees tend to change after they have been promoted. People act differently in different situations. The happy-go-lucky employee who is otherwise qualified for supervisory work may settle down once he has had taste of responsibility. The shy worker will often surprise everyone by the confidence and competence with which he takes over the supervisory role.

Here are some guiding questions to ask yourself when selecting a worker for supervisory training:

1. Does he know the techniques of his job well, either through training, experience, or preferably both?

2. Does he have a good knowledge of company policies and rules?

Whether a worker meets the two qualifications listed above usually depends on his length of time with the company. There are, however, other general qualities that have little to do with seniority. These are:

3. Can he give directions and instructions in such a way as to be acceptable in good spirit by subordinates?

4. Does he have the ability to follow the best method of operation and, more important, to improve on them?

5. Is he safety-conscious?

6. Is he cost-control and quality-control minded?

7. Can he keep records, plan jobs, and stick to time schedules?

Sometimes the company has policies that leave the supervisor little choice. He may be forced to choose a "stand-in" on the basis of seniority. Particularly is this true of civil service. Length of time on the job, job knowledge, or popularity with other employees alone are not a sound basis of selection. Therefore, where the supervisor does have freedom of choice, it is a mistake to turn the important business of choosing an understudy or successor into a seniority or popularity contest. The supervisor may be tempted to do this in the belief that choosing the oldest employee or the best-liked will help avoid resentment and envy on the part of other workers. Ill feelings will be stirred up, no matter who is chosen. Instead of trying to please everybody, the supervisor's basic consideration should be, "Who is the best man for the job?"

In developing a "stand-in," try to follow the same training principles discussed in the chapter on training. The new assistant can only learn by doing. If you've been a supervisor for a long time, it is only normal for you to feel reluctant about trusting him with your responsibilities. You will have to curb this tendency. If the understudy is to learn, he must make mistakes. If he is to have confidence in himself, you must show that you have confidence in him. Harsh criticism can destroy all the confidence he has built up. Training should be a daily affair. Give him a chance to practice at least one new supervisory task each working day. As he becomes more reliable and makes fewer mistakes, correction and protection should taper off.

A few of the larger companies have formal programs to develop supervisory material. Theoretical courses are helpful. But they should be supplemented by daily on-the-job training and experience. Supervisory material can't be developed by the use of charts, written tests, or "paper" courses alone. An employee must be given a chance to supervise if he is to learn to be a supervisor.

Here, briefly, are five rules for developing potential supervisors. You will note they are similar to those given in the chapter on instruction.

1. Delegate supervisory tasks to the trainee to *prime* the learning process.

2. Performance by the trainee, whether good or bad, must be reviewed periodically.

3. Show you have confidence in the trainee.

4. Be patient and give the trainee a chance to explain what he is doing.

5. Set a standard for the trainee. Make perfectly clear what you expect of him. The goals set should be targets that the trainee can reach or almost reach on a short-range basis. Gradually, as these standards are attained, raise the goals. The training then becomes a process where definite improvements can be seen and measured.

PLANNING YOUR WORK

Many difficulties stem from lack of supervisory planning or poor planning. These include waste of materials, poor quality and low output, high accident rates, and people working at cross purposes. Job planning is solving a problem and putting the solution to work. This applies whether the task is planning a new powerhouse, planning the day-to-day work of a clerical office, or distributing jobs in a radio and television repair shop. Six steps to follow in planning your work are:

1. Define the objective.
2. Collect available information.
3. Evaluate the data.
4. Prepare a plan of action.
5. Carry out the plan of action.
6. Check results.

Here is a convenient check list to use in your job planning:

— Assemble blueprints, plans, and other paper instructions.
— Make certain all necessary materials will be on hand.
— Check up on shortages of material or changes in material specifications.
— Estimate the number of workers needed.
— Estimate the tools and equipment needed.
— Estimate the time required.
— Examine the job site.
— Notify other work units or departments involved.
— Select the best-qualified workers for the job at hand.
— Make sure each employee you've chosen will be available.
— Give job instructions on the job site.
— Check your material list to make certain all materials have been delivered at the job site.
— Locate missing material, if any.
— Keep informed on the job's progress.

An important part of job planning is to plan to stay with the job, to check it, to keep posted on new developments. In other words, plan your work and work your plan.

How To Give Orders

Verbal orders. Most workers understand that they are paid to follow and carry out orders promptly. Generally they are willing to do this if they feel that the orders are consistent with their jobs and given in an acceptable manner. The wise supervisor issues orders with as little display of authority as possible. Simple verbal orders can often be given by asking a question that acts as a reminder. For example, a worker approaches a grinding wheel to smooth off the burr on the end of a newly-cut pipe section. The supervisor notes that his safety goggles are in his pocket. He asks, "Are your goggles in good shape?" The verbal order is conveyed in the form of a friendly reminder.

All verbal orders should be stated clearly and in simple terms. There should be no question as to *who is to do what and when.* Before assigning a specific job, decide who is best qualified to do it. Whenever possible, assign a specific time and place to do the job and state the procedure to be followed. Occasionally you will have to issue an order that is unusual or calls for an employee to do something that is not routine. Explain the reasons behind the order so that you may avoid misunderstanding or resistance.

Verbal orders can be issued as *commands,* which call for immediate and unquestioning compliance; *directions,* which are detailed explanations usually used for inexperienced workers; or *suggestions,* either in the form of a question or a gentle reminder for the experienced employee. Commands, which clearly imply the supervisor's authority should be used sparingly. They should be restricted to urgent situations.

Whether orders are given as commands, directions, or suggestions, the worker should clearly understand:

Why it is to be done.
What is to be done.
Where it is to be done.
When it is to be done.
How it is to be done.

Written orders. Although most of the orders you issue will be verbal, there will be times when written orders are necessary. This may be in cases where it is inconvenient or impossible to communicate with each worker individually, or the order is too long and involved to be given by word of mouth.

In many cases a supervisor often tries to show off his command of the English language when he puts an order in writing. For some reason or other he writes in technical and complicated terms way above the head of the average employee. This causes misunderstanding and confusion and leads to errors.

The following sign appeared in a small southern city:

"Notice to the Public — All persons will please take notice that it is prejudicial to the health of the community to expectorate on the sidewalks, and the general public is respectfully requested to refrain from this practice."

Compare this to the simple, yet effective: "Please don't spit!"

All written orders should be *Complete, Concise, Clear, Correct, Friendly.* Obviously material written on the level of a scientific journal is ineffective with people whose regular reading diet may be Batman. Aim your written orders at the educational level of your employees. Here are four good rules for making your written message clear and effective:

1. *Eliminate useless words.*

Instead of "You are advised that the schedule should be sent directly to this office as promptly as possible . . . ," write, "The schedule should be sent to this office promptly . . ."

2. *Use concise expressions.* Instead of "The company is of the opinion that . . . ," write, "We believe . . ."

3. *Use a word for a phrase.* Instead of "In view of the fact that . . . ," write, "Because . . ."

4. *Avoid repetition.* Instead of "The study is nearly completed at the present time . . . ," write, "The study is nearly completed . . ."

Reminder: Use all the words you will need to carry your message clearly and correctly, *but use no more.*

Cost Control

Most companies today have cost accountants and elaborate systems for analyzing costs and setting up budgets. If the organization's policy is to give each supervisor a regular budget to follow, the supervisor's main concern with cost control will be to keep within his budget. The system has several faults. It puts pressure on the supervisor and creates irritability. If the budget is too "tight," the tendency is to try to beat it by overestimating costs, borrowing from other departments, and similar arrangements.

In general, the cost-conscious supervisor can help keep company costs down by doing a good supervisory job. Accidents and labor turnover, for example, are always costly. Breaking in a new employee may cost more than $500.00. Inefficient placement of workers and failure to train workers properly results in poor quality. Other factors that increase company costs are excessive waste; damage to equipment; a failure to meet schedules; and excessive absenteeism.

QUALITY CONTROL

Because of increasing business and industrial competition, companies today give top priority to the problem of controlling the quality of goods and services. However, just as important as *improving* quality is *standardizing* quality. Uniform products and services are necessary if advertising is to be effective and consumer demand maintained. Business and industrial organizations, therefore, must keep quality within a given range. Quality cannot be too poor, or people will stop buying. It cannot be so high as to make the cost of production prohibitive. In most cases the real problem is to keep quality above the minimum level rather than below the maximum.

To do this large companies use "statistical quality control" systems. Trained technicians are employed to "spot check" samples of the product or service for defects of materials, equipment, and workmanship.

Controlling quality is also the responsibility of supervision. The alert supervisor can prevent flaws in the first place — namely, during the production stage. Except in the case of sabotage, defects of quality are unplanned. They are *accidents*. In the chapter on accident control we described how accidents can lead to employee injuries. Because accidents can also lead to quality defects, it is clear that in quality control the supervisor can use the same type of treatment he employs to prevent job injuries. Human failure causes 80 per cent of the injury-producing accidents, and mechanical failure accounts for 20 per cent. The same has been found to hold true for accidents of *quality*. By eliminating human and mechanical failure wherever possible, the supervisor not only prevents employee injuries but plays an important role in quality control.

PERSONNEL DUTIES

Most organizations of any size have personnel or employee relations departments. These are not large enough to do a complete, or even an adequate job of personnel administration. Each supervisor must serve as the day-to-day personnel man for his group. He must orient new employees; explain wage and salary changes; take care of transfers, promotions, and merit ratings; adjust minor complaints; and assist in the initial handling of major grievances.

When these routine matters come up, the good supervisor doesn't try to "pass the buck" to an already understaffed personnel office. It creates the feeling among his men that he is weak and doesn't have any authority on his own. To protect his status as a leader he accepts these jobs cheerfully, even enthusiastically. This doesn't mean the supervisor makes promises he doesn't have the power to fulfill.

Nor does he mislead the employee with "half-promises" in order to appear friendly. Too often the anxious employee twists a half-promise into a full-promise in his own mind. Later, when his hopes are dashed, no explanation by the supervisor — for example, "I said I would try" — will soothe the worker's feelings or help raise his injured morale. Make your position a clear and definite one from the start.

In personnel work the supervisor, as in his other functions, has opportunity, authority, and responsibility. His authority in personnel matters goes up to a certain point, usually set by top management. He should not hesitate to consult with his superior or with the personnel department when a situation arises that is complicated, unusual, or beyond his power to settle alone. This is especially true in the case of the employee who remains a disciplinary "problem" when all other constructive approaches have failed, or when a serious violation occurs such as drinking on the job, immoral acts, assault, theft, sabotage, or serious safety or sanitary violations.

PUBLIC RELATIONS

Companies spend huge sums each year on "public relations." The purpose is to create a favorable public attitude toward the organization — its policies, products, and services. This is partially done by sending "releases" to the press on company news. The policy has its origin in the simple idea that "What benefits the community benefits us." Good public relations must be practiced on a day-to-day basis. It is not enough for a company to hold an "open house" for the general public or to help in a community chest drive once a year. Little everyday actions — whether a secretary is courteous when answering the phone, or a receptionist is helpful toward visitors — are just as important. It is not unusual for a casual visitor who had a single, unhappy experience with a gruff plant protection man at the gate, to come away with an unfavorable impression of the organization as a whole.

If the company is located in a small town the after-hours activities of its employees become especially important. When a worker participates in community activities, is friendly with his neighbors, and speaks highly of his company, he helps build good public relations for the organization among his friends, relatives, and acquaintances.

The supervisor, who, as a member of management is closely identified as an "official" representative of the company, plays an even more significant part in creating a favorable climate of public opinion. He should recognize the fact that he has a personal stake in his company — that his fortunes are determined by the success of his employer. He should be courteous in all his contacts with the public, and seek to become an active, respected member of his community.

A supervisor who is a good citizen is a good public relations representative for his employer. Since he can do much to influence the behavior of his men, he should also impress on them the necessity for courtesy and good citizenship. The public-relations-conscious supervisor can thus make a vital contribution to his company's welfare.

CHECK YOUR SUPERVISORY
KNOW-HOW

THE FOLLOWING PAGES contain a self-appraisal test drawn from the material in this book. The purpose of the test is to help you review important supervisory principles you read about earlier; to give you a better awareness of your supervisory methods and techniques; and to help you determine just where you need improvement.

Answer each question by putting a check under "Yes" if you agree, or under "No" if you disagree. Then check your answers against those beginning on page 191.

	YES	No
1. Consult with your workers on tough jobs.	☐	☐
2. How long a worker is absent is more important than how often.	☐	☐
3. Observance of safety rules is up to the worker.	☐	☐
4. If an employee has a complaint, walk away from him.	☐	☐
5. Train a worker for speed and then pick up his errors.	☐	☐
6. A foreman is judged entirely on his group's production.	☐	☐

	YES	No
7. Make exceptions to company rules.	☐	☐
8. A worker's personal life is of no interest to you as supervisor.	☐	☐
9. Give workers advance notice of changes.	☐	☐
10. Look the other way when first violations occur.	☐	☐
11. A fast learner always makes a good worker.	☐	☐
12. Favorite workers should get the "breaks."	☐	☐
13. New employees learn best by just watching.	☐	☐
14. Workers are supposed to ask questions about the job.	☐	☐
15. It's your duty to interfere in workers' arguments.	☐	☐
16. Transfer unhappy but capable workers to other jobs.	☐	☐
17. Slow workers should be threatened with dismissal.	☐	☐
18. It's a good idea to train a capable worker to cover your job.	☐	☐
19. If a gripe is lengthy, cut it short.	☐	☐
20. Decisions should be made quickly.	☐	☐
21. The supervisor should be blamed for accidents.	☐	☐
22. The best worker usually makes the best foreman.	☐	☐

	YES	No
23. If you can't settle matters with a worker, take him to your boss.	☐	☐
24. It's a good idea to occasionally buy some of your men a beer after work.	☐	☐
25. If asked, give your opinion on a worker's personal problems.	☐	☐
26. Most accidents are unavoidable.	☐	☐
27. An employee is interested in money, not in credit or praise.	☐	☐
28. What a worker thinks about job conditions is often as important as what he does about them.	☐	☐
29. A supervisor should stand up for his men.	☐	☐
30. Employees usually understand the importance of their jobs.	☐	☐
31. After reprimanding a worker, be tough with him.	☐	☐
32. An intelligent worker is often bored with a simple job.	☐	☐
33. Each worker should be allowed to develop his own work methods.	☐	☐
34. Explain to each employee why his work is important and how it fits in with the work of the rest of the department and with the purpose of the entire organization.	☐	☐
35. Supervisory skills can usually be learned.	☐	☐
36. Blame human nature when things go wrong in your department.	☐	☐

	Yes	No
37. A supervisor should admit to errors.	☐	☐
38. You should be willing to lose your best worker to a better job.	☐	☐
39. Accept criticism directed at yourself.	☐	☐
40. Always let a worker know when he starts "slipping."	☐	☐
41. A good boss is always friendly to the workers.	☐	☐
42. The best educated workers make the best employees.	☐	☐
43. When breaking in a new employee, turn him over to a good worker for training.	☐	☐
44. The foreman or supervisor represents management to the worker.	☐	☐
45. A supervisor is supposed to watch every worker every minute of the working day.	☐	☐
46. People work better when a definite goal is set.	☐	☐
47. No one likes a "strict" boss.	☐	☐
48. A majority of your workers are stupid.	☐	☐
49. Instructing or correcting a worker once or twice should be enough.	☐	☐
50. If a worker doesn't understand a job, he will ask for help.	☐	☐

ANSWERS TO
SELF-APPRAISAL TEST

1. *Consult with your workers on tough jobs.*
   YES. Consultation develops better understanding between supervisor and workers, and leads to more willing cooperation. A supervisor can often obtain valuable ideas from his subordinates.

2. *How long a worker is absent is more important than how often.*
   NO. A long absence usually results from illness or other unavoidable causes. Frequent absenteeism, on the other hand, may be a sign of improper attitude and should be investigated. It also makes it more difficult for management to keep production rolling along without interruptions.

3. *Observance of safety rules is up to the worker.*
   NO. The supervisor has the authority and opportunity — and therefore the responsibility — for seeing that all company rules, including safety regulations, are enforced.

4. *If an employee has a complaint, walk away from him.*
   NO. The worker will simply become more resentful. The supervisor should try to arrange for a private session. He should be a sympathetic listener and give the worker a chance to get the grievance off his chest.

5. *Train a worker for speed and then pick up his errors.*
   NO. The employee should be trained to do the job accurately in the beginning. Speed will de-

velop afterwards provided he has already learned to do it correctly. Setting a quota or goal will aid learning.

6. *A foreman is judged entirely on his group's production.*

NO. Achieving a good departmental production record is important. But helping out another department benefits the company as a whole and is recognized by the company's executives as a strong point in the supervisor's favor. The company head is more concerned with coordination and cooperation on his staff than with individual productive ability.

7. *Make exceptions to company rules.*

YES. Special cases require special handling. Emergencies and new situations often arise that call for modifying the company rules. If the supervisor doesn't have the authority to alter the rules on his own, he should consult with his superiors.

8. *A worker's personal life is of no interest to you as supervisor.*

NO. The worker's health, household, financial, and other personal problems affect his on-the-job performance. Therefore, they are the concern of the supervisor.

9. *Give workers advance notice of changes.*

YES. It prevents the worker from developing a feeling that he is "being pushed around" without being told why. It is surprising how often an employee will mistakenly think that a sudden, unexplained reassignment means the supervisor is dissatisfied with his work.

10. *Look the other way when first violations occur.*
NO. Once the supervisor ignores a violation the workers interpret it to mean that he will tolerate the same violation in the future. A pattern is thus set and other employees are tempted to follow the example. If the supervisor tries to correct the violation later, a worker will resent it much more than if he had received correction in the beginning.

11. *A fast learner always makes a good worker.*
NO. Slow learners often become good, steady, dependable workers. Although learning speed is important because it saves the company time and money, the supervisor should remember that it isn't essential. A fast learner may turn out to be careless and undependable.

12. *Favorite workers should get the "breaks."*
NO. Giving favorite workers the "breaks" leaves the supervisor open to charges of favoritism. It leads to resentment and poor morale among the other employees. The supervisor should spread the "breaks" around by a rotation method. He should also keep a written record so members of his group can see for themselves that he isn't playing favorites.

13. *New employees learn best by just watching.*
NO. Breaking in a new worker just by having him watch others is the old-fashioned way. Educators have found that a much more effective method is for the employee to *learn by doing*. This system calls for the supervisor to 1) prepare the worker; 2) instruct him; 3) have him apply the instruction; 4) check or test the worker.

14. *Workers are supposed to ask questions about the job.*
YES. An employee always works better when he knows the *whys* of his job — why he is supposed to do a certain thing and why he is supposed to do it in a certain way. It prevents him from feeling he is left out of things and that there are family "top secrets" with which he isn't trusted.

15. *It's your duty to interfere in workers' arguments.*
YES. Anything that interferes with the smooth operation of the department is the supervisor's responsibility. Arguments affect output. The supervisor should try to promote group harmony by acting as a moderator and using on-the-job control. If necessary, he should use discipline.

16. *Transfer unhappy but capable workers to other jobs.*
YES. A good employee may be unhappy in his job because of a personality clash, boredom, or for a number of other reasons. In some cases the supervisor should try to reassign him rather than keep him in the same job where his continued discontent eventually will "ruin" him as a worker for the company.

17. *Slow workers should be threatened with dismissal.*
NO. There is usually a reason why a worker is slow. The supervisor should look for that reason. He may have to encourage greater effort on the part of the employee, work with him to improve his skill, or get him to assume a better attitude towards his work.

18. *It's a good idea to train a capable worker to cover your job.*
YES. By training a competent replacement, the supervisor will be giving encouragement to his subordinates. He will also have someone to replace him so that production won't suffer when he is ill or called away. At the same time it frees him for promotion or other opportunities. The company executives know that moving him up will not disrupt company organization since he has broken in someone to take over his old job.

19. *If a gripe is lengthy, cut it short.*
NO. The supervisor should not cut a gripe short. A full hearing is important since it helps the worker "get it off his chest" and calms him down. Then, too, important information concerning working conditions or employee morale usually comes at the end of a griping session.

20. *Decisions should be made quickly.*
NO. If it is vital to make a quick decision, make it to the best of your ability. Otherwise, take your time. Look at a question from all angles before making up your mind about it.

21. *The supervisor should be blamed for accidents.*
NO. The supervisor should not be "blamed" for accidents. But he is responsible for investigating, determining the cause, and taking the steps necessary to see that the accident is not repeated. He can be held accountable by the "big boss." Accountability and responsibility differ from "blame." Blame implies that the supervisor was negligent or permitted a recurrence of the accident.

22. *The best worker usually makes the best foreman.*
NO. A good worker doesn't necessarily make a good supervisor. A supervisor's most important qualification is leadership ability. An efficient worker may or may not be a good leader. Also, he may lack the ability to plan, instruct, improve methods, accept responsibility, keep records, or cooperate with other staff members and supervisors.

23. *If you can't settle matters with a worker, take him to your boss.*
YES. Taking a worker to your boss when you can't settle matters with him yourself shows him you're not a "dictator." As a result, he will go *through* you instead of over your head if he wants to appeal a decision in the future.

24. *It's a good idea to occasionally buy some of your men a beer after work.*
NO. The supervisor who is "too friendly" after working hours may find it hard to enforce discipline on the job. If he associates only with a certain few of his group, he may be accused of favoritism. Friendliness is a good quality in a boss. But it should be kept on a uniform level and shown to all employees alike.

25. *If asked, give your opinion on a worker's personal problems.*
NO. When dealing with a worker's personal problems, the supervisor should limit himself to sympathizing, asking questions and providing factual information such as the name of a social agency. He should not give his own opinions as to what the employee should or should not do.

Rather, he should try to get the worker himself to arrive at the correct decision.

26. *Most accidents are unavoidable.*
NO.   Surveys and statistics show that more than 60 per cent of accidents in the average plant can be avoided in actual practice.

27. *An employee is interested in money, not in credit or praise.*
NO.   In addition to a paycheck, the average worker wants 1) to feel that his job is secure and offers room for advancement; 2) good working conditions; 3) to get along with his boss; 4) to feel he is doing important work.

28. *What a worker thinks about job conditions is often as important as what he does about them.*
YES.   Employees may be resentful about conditions on the job for some time before they decide to do something about it.   A good supervisor learns to *sense* low morale or friction among his men and tries to clear up the trouble before it leads to absenteeism, strikes and other serious problems.

29. *A supervisor should stand up for his men.*
YES.   A supervisor who shows that he is willing to stand up for the interests of his men develops loyalty, teamwork, cooperation, and high morale.   He will win the respect of management.

30. *Employees usually understand the importance of their jobs.*
NO.   In most cases the worker doesn't relate his own individual job to the over-all picture.   A supervisor must educate his men to see their jobs as important parts of the company operation.

31. *After reprimanding a worker, be tough with him.*
NO. If a worker thinks you bear a grudge against him for a past mistake, he will feel persecuted and resentful. He may even try to "get even" by laying down on the job or breaking other company rules.

32. *An intelligent worker is often bored with a simple job.*
YES. An intelligent worker is quickly bored with a simple, routine job. His efficiency and morale suffer. The supervisor should give him a chance at more complicated work that challenges his ability, provides interest, and avoids monotony and fatigue.

33. *Each worker should be allowed to develop his own work methods.*
NO. Individual work methods lead to confusion and inefficiency. Once a standard procedure is set, every worker should be required to follow it. However, when an employee suggests a system that he feels is better, it should be examined and considered. If it is an improvement over the regular method, it should be standardized for the entire company.

34. *Explain to each employee why his work is important and how it fits in with the work of the rest of the department and with the purpose of the entire organization.*
YES. Many people suffer from a feeling that what they are doing is not "important." They need to be told that the whole organization depends on the proper execution of their work. It is because this kind of assurance is so seldom

given that many employees show an attitude of indifference which reflects itself in the quality of their work.

35. *Supervisory skills can usually be learned.*
YES. Human beings aren't born with supervisory skills. These skills must be learned and developed. Of course, as in other fields, there are individuals who show a special talent for supervisory work. But even for them, it is a matter of training and experience at the beginning.

36. *Blame human nature when things go wrong in your department.*
NO. Don't blame all your troubles on people's personalities and attitudes. Many conflicts arise from misunderstandings about job responsibilities — from an overlapping of jurisdiction among employees or among supervisors. Clear directions and patient reinstruction may be indicated.

37. *A supervisor should admit to errors.*
YES. A supervisor who openly admits his mistakes sets a good example for his subordinates. They are less likely to try to hide their own errors — a practice that is costly. Also, since the worker realizes no one in infallible, he usually respects a boss who doesn't pretend that he never makes mistakes.

38. *You should be willing to lose your best worker to a better job.*
YES. A supervisor who is willing to see a good worker rewarded—even if it means losing him—encourages the others to do their best. It shows his subordinates that he is fair. In effect, losing

the services of a good man through promotion pays off in higher group morale and efficiency.

39. *Accept criticism directed at yourself.*
YES. Train yourself to keep an open mind to criticism even when it may seem unjust. Such ability commands the respect of others and enables you to pick out the points which you can use for your own development. Cooperate with your associates and superiors in giving them the opportunity to straighten you out when you are off the track. They are training you for future responsibility, just as you are trying to develop your own men. Stand up for your rights when you know your position is sound, but do it without getting hot under the collar.

40. *Always let a worker know when he starts "slipping."*
YES. It is only fair to the worker to let him know when he's slipping so he can do something about it. It gives the supervisor a chance to talk things over and find out whether the trouble lies with the employee or the job itself. The sooner the supervisor brings up the matter, the sooner and easier the situation can be corrected.

41. *A good boss is always friendly to the workers.*
NO. An employee's behavior doesn't always call for "friendly" treatment. Just as a parent is occasionally forced to use discipline on a child, the supervisor is sometimes required to display his authority. There are always a few workers who assume the "always friendly" supervisor is an "easy" supervisor, and they try to get away with as much as possible.

42. *The best educated workers make the best employees.*
    NO. The best educated worker doesn't always make the best employee. In certain jobs, like engineering or accounting, the worker with educational training has an advantage. There are other factors that must be considered: reliability, practical experience, physical coordination, and the like.

43. *When breaking in a new employee, turn him over to a good worker for training.*
    NO. Training a new worker is the responsibility of the supervisor. It cannot be entrusted entirely to a subordinate. A competent worker may not be a competent teacher. However, this doesn't mean that the supervisor shouldn't call on experienced workers for occasional help in breaking in the newcomer.

44. *The foreman or supervisor represents management to the worker.*
    YES. The supervisor is the worker's contact with management and therefore represents the company to him.

45. *A supervisor is supposed to watch every worker every minute of the working day.*
    NO. It is physically impossible for the supervisor to watch every move every worker makes every minute of the working day. Even of he could, there would be no room for initiative on the part of the employee. The supervisor should spend his time observing and controlling each worker's repetitive habits, attitudes, and working practices.

46. *People work better when a definite goal is set.*
YES. The advantage of setting goals is that the worker gets a feeling of accomplishment and satisfaction if he reaches the goal.

47. *No one likes a "strict" boss.*
NO. Workers can like and respect a strict boss — provided he is fair and friendly as well as firm. The important thing is for the supervisor to be consistent in his behavior so that employees know what to expect. He cannot be liked if he is strict and unfriendly one day, and "easy" and friendly the next.

48. *A majority of your workers are stupid.*
NO. The supervisor who gets the feeling that most of his workers are stupid is really trying to alibi himself for doing a poor job of bossing. Experience shows that most groups of employees are of average intelligence — though some individual workers may be below or above average.

49. *Instructing or correcting a worker once or twice should be enough.*
NO. Some instructions or corrections may have to be repeated a dozen times or more before they become part of the employee's working habits. Of course, this doesn't refer to the worker who willfully commits serious violations.

50. *If a worker doesn't understand a job, he will ask for help.*
NO. The average worker prefers to bumble along, bluff, or get advice from co-workers — sometimes the wrong advice — rather than ask the supervisor for help. This is especially true of new workers who are afraid that the boss will

think they are incompetent if they ask him for help.

SCORING

The rating scale below is similar to that used by civil service commissions and many private firms to evaluate employees. Based on the average scores of several thousand men and women on the "first line operating supervisory" level such as foremen and office managers who have taken the test in the past, you may now compare your score.

To rate your own supervisory "know-how," add up your "correct" answers and allow one point for each.

Total Correct Answers

50-47	Excellent
47-40	Very Good
40-37	Good
37-30	Fair
30 or below	Poor

INDEX

A

Absenteeism, 41, 43, 71, 72, 157
  attitudes toward, 71
  control of, 71, 72
  solution for, 72
Accidents, 41, 73-94, 96
  causes of, 75, 77, 81-84, 86-88
  control of, 73-94
  cost of, 73, 74
  dealing with, 89
  kinds of, 80-84
  prevention of, 90-94
  remedies for, 88, 89
  reports on, 90
Allen, Dr. Charles R., and
  training, 98, 99
American Standards Association,
  and accident control, 81-84,
  86-88
Appreciation, and praise, 8, 14,
  18, 20, 34, 36, 37, 53, 110,
  147
Arguments, avoidance of, 28, 29,
  33, 52
Authority, channels of, 54, 55,
  97, 185

B

Behavior, laws of, 5

C

Challenges, kinds of, 36, 50
  use of, 35
Changes, handling of, 7
  institution of, 6
  preparation for, 46-48, 145
  resistance to, 6, 7, 13
Communications, company, 24,
  25, 55
Conference, conduct of, 15-21
  method, 14
  participation in, 18
  preparation for, 21
  reasons for failure of, 19, 20
  success of, 16
  topics for, 21
  types of, 15, 16
Consistency, 13, 63, 64, 67, 68
Cooling-Off Period, 29
Cooperation, 23-40, 162, 166
  barriers to, 25, 26
  benefits of, 29, 32, 34, 35, 39
  defined, 23
  future, 34, 36, 37
  in handling problems, 162
  on the job, 32
  value of, 23, 24
  voluntary nature of, 38
  ways of winning, 15, 27, 34,
  38
Cost Control, 183
Criticism, resentment of, 8, 14,
  29, 52

D

Discipline, 58-72
  consistency in, 63, 64, 67, 68
  forms of, 59
  necessity for, 63
  of employees, 58
  "tight vs. lax," 63-65

E

Efficiency Engineering, 122-126,
  145, 146
Ego Hunger, 7, 8
Employee, and personal problems, 119
  best use of, 49
  control of, 58
  output of, 42, 43
  performance, 4
  preparation for change, 46-48
  recognition of, 44
  screening, 49, 175
  testing, 49
  training, 95-119
  turnover, 12, 41, 43
Errors, admission of, 30
  avoidance of, 96, 110, 111

F

Favoritism, avoidance of, 50-52
Flow Diagram, 132-134, 142
Flow Process Chart, 130-147
  preparation of, 130-132
  use of, 134-142
Four-Step Method, 99, 100, 102,
  115, 117

Index

206